Halal Hustle

Unlocking the Muslim Entrepreneur
Mindset for Success in Business

SARAH GULFRAZ

Copyright © 2024 Sarah Gulfraz

Sarah Gulfraz has asserted her right to be identified as the author of this Work in accordance with the Copyright, Designs and Patents Act 1988.

All rights reserved.

No portion of this book may be reproduced in any form, stored in a retrieval system, stored in a database, or published/transmitted in any form or by any means, electronic, mechanical, photocopying, recording or otherwise, without prior written permission of the publisher.

Dedication

~ **Bismillah** ~

May Allah (swt) accept our efforts and grant us success in this life and the next. Ameen.

In dedication to my loving family and all their support.

Contents

Introduction	1
1. Defining Islamic Entrepreneurship	3
2. Faith-Based Leadership and Vision	20
3. Entrepreneurial Resilience and Perseverance	34
4. Islamic Business Ethics and Integrity	46
5. Entrepreneurial Mindset and Innovation	59
6. Financial Management and Risk-Taking	85
7. Social Impact and Community Engagement	91
8. Networking and Collaborative Partnerships	97
9. Future Trends in Islamic Entrepreneurship	104
10. Final Thoughts	113
Find Out More	116

Introduction

Entrepreneurship is the primary pillar of economic growth and development. Nations with solid entrepreneurial cultures see exponential growth in all spheres of the economy, including employment, income, technical advancement, wealth distribution equity, prosperity, and social and economic stability. As a religion, Islam encourages entrepreneurship due to the significant positive impacts these activities have on economies and society.

Islamic beliefs and principles serve as the foundation for Islamic entrepreneurship. Islam offers moral and ethical precepts for living that apply to all facets of life, but particularly to conducting business. Religion significantly influences national economic policy and corporate operations.

Islam is a complete lifestyle; there is no distinction between religion and commerce. It has a unique culture of entrepreneurship and business tenets drawn from the Quran and Hadith. Islam is crucial in fostering an entrepreneurial mindset that will increase commercial activity. Examples of this include the Prophet Muhammad (PBUH) and his companions. Islam always encourages all Muslims to be creative and engaged business owners.

This book is intended for readers curious about Islamic entrepreneurship. It is designed to help them grasp all the essential aspects of building a successful entrepreneurship mindset. Whether an aspiring entrepreneur, business leader, or start-up manager, this book will equip the reader with the necessary foundational knowledge.

Dissecting the features and dynamics of Islamic entrepreneurship, leadership, struggle, morality, creativity, and community involvement, it offers a comprehensive picture of a man for whom business life is sacred and divine.

Thus, Islamic entrepreneurship is not solely about profit-making; it is a business based on the Islamic principles of ethics, philanthropy, and duty to society. As borrowed from Islamic teachings and exemplified by the leadership of Prophet Muhammad (PBUH), aspiring business leaders should strive towards beneficial goals under divine guidance with persistence and determination in facing adversities.

This guide is a powerful message encouraging readers to find inspiration that transcends the general idea of business success. From experienced entrepreneurs to budding startups, readers will easily be encouraged and guided to engage in Islamic entrepreneurship while contributing to society's economic growth and welfare. Let's dive in!

Chapter One

Defining Islamic Entrepreneurship

These days, the rise of entrepreneurship contributes significantly to the economic expansion of both developed and developing countries. This word is often synonymous with "innovation that benefits society" and "job creation." Seasoned business entrepreneurs belong to small and medium-sized enterprises (MSMEs).

Business owners operate in several global economic domains. The halal industry, representing the global Islamic economy, is one of the fastest-growing markets. The leading participants in this global halal business are halal entrepreneurs, sometimes known as "halalpreneurs".

Many academics, businesspeople, researchers, and experts from around the globe have characterised entrepreneurship. Most economies worldwide have adopted and employed the phrase in the same manner. However, the meaning of "entrepreneurship" varies across conventional and Islamic economies. Although the concept and scope of activities are identical, Islam gives it a different connotation and calls it "halalpreneurship".

The word "halal" is an Arabic or Quranic term that refers to an Islamic way of life and whose literal meaning is "permissible" or "lawful." This implies that the term's meaning applies to all aspects of human behaviour, whether social, personal, professional, cultural, or political. From an economic standpoint, "halal industry" has been used to refer to the Islamic economy.

Entrepreneurship is an essential part of life and is also intrinsic to Islam. Known as halalpreneurship, it operates within the boundaries of Shariah, encompassing *Aqidah*, *Fiqh*, *Akhlaq*, ensuring that all activities adhere to Islamic law.

Islam views halalpreneurship as the earthly equivalent of the duty of the caliph, or Khalifah. Worshipping Allah (SWT) and advancing global development and prosperity are the two main goals of Khalifah. Such a role entails entrepreneurial activities that advance the welfare of society, the global community, and humanity as a whole.

> *Allah says: "And that man shall have nothing but what he strives for" (Quran, 53:39)*

Labour and activities form the basis of the world. God gave each of his creations certain tools so they might benefit from and avoid their weaknesses based on this sequence. Humans, the most complex species on Earth, require more actions than any other to meet its many demands and preserve the family and society.

It has been said by Jafar al-Sadiq (a): "O you Mufaddal know; God make it difficult to gain bread, and without administration and movement it cannot be available," meaning that he will be able to obtain a job through it that will shield him from the adverse effects of unemployment, which equates to stupidity and foolishness.

Being an entrepreneur is a challenging, exciting, and often unexpected journey. Creating something new and worthwhile takes vision, bravery, and persistence. If you are a Muslim business entrepreneur, you will likely encounter more ethical dilemmas in reconciling Islamic values with financial success.

In this guide, we will talk about applying your Islamic principles to your commercial activities without compromising your morals, ethics, or beliefs. We present an introduction to entrepreneurship from an Islamic perspective and how Muslim entrepreneurs can build a business model. We will examine current literature, passages from the Holy Quran, Hadith (sayings of the Prophet Muhammad (PBUH)), and sunnah (practice) on Islamic entrepreneurship. Keep reading to gain insightful knowledge about Islamic entrepreneurship!

Understanding the Concept of Islamic Entrepreneurship

Entrepreneurship is an integral part of Islamic economics and an inseparable part of Islamic finance. It involves the pursuit of economic opportunity and the deployment of halal resources to harness halal opportunities observed in the environment.

Prophet Muhammad (SAW) and his companions, the Tabi'een, exemplified Muslim entrepreneurship. Since then, numerous successful Muslim entrepreneurs have emerged, as Islam consistently encourages all Muslims to be creative, innovative and active in the field of entrepreneurship.

The search for financial opportunities and the application of halal means to seize halal opportunities found in the surroundings is known as entrepreneurship. Both Islamic finance and Islamic economics are inextricably linked to entrepreneurship.

The Prophet Muhammad (PBUH) and his companions were the ideal Muslim businesspeople. Following their example, several prosperous Muslim businesspeople emerged, as Islam consistently promotes innovation, creativity, and active participation in commerce.

Islamic teachings encourage entrepreneurs to engage in business ventures such as purchasing, selling, providing services, and making goods. According to the teachings of the Quran and Shariah law, Muslims have two primary obligations: Ibadah and Khalifah.

Ibadah involves acts of worship and devotion, including Salat (prayer), Sawm (fasting), Zakat (charity), and the Hajj (pilgrimage). Under the system of Khalifah (viceregency), Muslims are tasked with governing, developing people and resources, pursuing riches, and working hard and lawfully to sustain themselves, their families, and society. Legal business ventures are an expansion of Ibadah.

Islam has unique entrepreneurial traits and tenets for conducting business, which are derived from the Quran and the Hadith.

> *Allah the Almighty says, "Business is lawful for you"*
> *(Quran, 2:275)*

Islam, being a complete and comprehensive way of life (Quran, 5:3), strongly promotes the growth of trade, commerce, industry, and agriculture as these endeavours increase and mobilise resources to meet the needs of the population.

Islamic entrepreneurship is seen as a critical component of business prosperity and longevity. It contributes significantly to both national and global economic growth and development.

In Islam, the brotherhood forms a sense of solidarity and bond, enabling everyone to collaborate as a team. During the time of Prophet Muhammad (PBUH) and his companions, cooperative and collaborative work both inside and between teams produced strong forces for inventive social change. Islam has always encouraged people to start their own businesses and never stop seeking Allah's blessings. In Islam, commerce and entrepreneurship are highly valuable.

Islam encourages entrepreneurship because of the tremendous contribution that entrepreneurial endeavours make to economies and society. Nations with strong entrepreneurial cultures see exponential growth in all spheres of the economy, including employment, income, technical advancement, equitable income distribution, prosperity, and social and economic stability.

Islamic entrepreneurship is more dynamic and all-encompassing than traditional entrepreneurship. Unlike traditional business, which concentrates exclusively on financial gains, Islamic entrepreneurship handles social and economic activities equally.

> *"That, whoever does justice, male or female, as one who believes we will provide him a comfortable life," Allah SWT stated in the Quran. We will provide them with encouragement based on our greater understanding of their prior performance (Quran: 16:97)*

Muslims are expected to earn a living in accordance with Shariah laws and the teachings of the Quran. Islam emphasises the value of being involved in business ventures that benefit society as a whole, and many of the restrictions imposed on Muslim entrepreneurs are intended to minimise activities that could harm the community. It is thought by Muslims that taking up entrepreneurial endeavours fulfils their Islamic duty to appease Allah. Islam supports and facilitates entrepreneurial activity while influencing it at various economic levels.

According to Islam, an individual's main goal plays a significant role in defining their character and motivations when launching a business. Thus, ambition plays a crucial role in Islam. The Prophet Muhammad asserts that every deed and every action is motivated by a certain intention.

> Additionally, Prophet Muhammad stated that *"Each person will be given the reward in accordance with*

what he has willed" and that "the reward for deeds should be based on the specific intention" (Bukhari)

Islam provides a structure for behaviour, and a sense of being that satisfies both physical and spiritual needs. Its moral and ethical principles encourage achieving grandeur of spirit and tolerance, equipping individuals with the resilience to navigate life's challenges. Islam fosters a cohesive society characterised by a brotherhood endowed with social responsibility, as well as a sense of self-respect and familial values for the individual.

In Islam, starting a business or start-up is not the ultimate aim; rather, what matters most is how a person gets there and the positive impact they generate with the profits. Since entrepreneurship is about creating value, these principles are fundamental to Islamic beliefs. Muslim entrepreneurs should focus on generating value for economic growth, wealth creation, and social impact. Entrepreneurship empowers an individual financially so they can share it with others.

In sum, Islam has a unique place for entrepreneurs and entrepreneurship, with the al-Quran and Hadith as the foundation for an Islamic business plan. Islam views all aspects of life, including business, as all-encompassing. Consequently, entrepreneurship in Islam encompasses all facets of life, whether for this world or the next.

Defining Islamic entrepreneurship and its significance

The process of launching a company or similar organisation is known as entrepreneurship. It is an entrepreneur's inseparable process of spotting market possibilities, gathering the necessary resources to go after, and making the investments required to take advantage of the prospects for long-term profits.

Within the framework of Islam, the primary goal of a Muslim's business endeavours must be to please Allah. This entails conducting business in accordance with the ethical and moral principles of Islamic practices, meeting one's religious obligations, and positively impacting society as a whole. Islamic entrepreneurship places a strong emphasis on fulfilling religious duties; as a result, success is determined not only by financial gain but also by ethical considerations, which, under Islamic belief, may earn the entrepreneur benefits in the afterlife.

A suitable portion of the population engages in entrepreneurial endeavours of their own volition and initiative. In addition to fostering self-reliance, entrepreneurship contributes to the efficient operation of national economies.

As mentioned, Islam is an all-encompassing lifestyle, and no distinction is made between religion and commerce. It has a unique culture of entrepreneurship and tenets for conducting business drawn from the Quran and Hadith. A component of Islamic business and economics is entrepreneurship.

Islamic entrepreneurship is the basis for each entrepreneur's unique interactions with Allah and other people. By embracing the concept of Taqwa, entrepreneurs can develop qualities aligned with Islamic principles derived from the Quran and Sunnah. The teachings of Islam are a valuable resource for achieving great success in the world of entrepreneurship.

Islam encourages all Muslims to lead active, diligent lives—qualities that are common among entrepreneurs and company owners. Islam's core principles advocate prosperity by wisely using God's resources. For this reason, the concept of both haram and halal for Muslims is explicitly classified by Islamic law.

To put it briefly, Islamic entrepreneurship is founded on Islamic law and principles. Entrepreneurs who wholeheartedly adhere to these laws and concepts are deemed to be Muslim entrepreneurs, also known as Muslimpreneurs.

Sayings of the Prophet Muhammad (PBUH) include: "A truthful merchant will be raised on the Day of Judgment along with the truthful and the martyrs" and "Righteous businessmen will be the first to enter paradise".

The Prophet was also a businessman before he declared himself a prophet. He established himself as a prosperous businessman by virtue of his honesty, intelligence, and trustworthiness and was given the nickname *Al-Amin* ("the trustworthy").

In Islam, entrepreneurship is encouraged not only in men but also in women. Hazrat Khadija (ra), the Prophet Muhammad's (PBUH) wife, is a notable example of a prosperous businesswoman. May Allah be pleased with her! As Islam is seen as a "religion of entrepreneurs" in and of itself, promoting and enabling risk-taking, creativity, and, above all, the ability to recognise the finest business opportunities.

Importance of faith-based principles in entrepreneurial endeavours

In Islam, faith-based principles have a significant role in entrepreneurial endeavours, shaping both the ethical framework and practical approaches to business. The confluence of corporate acumen alongside personal faith is characterised by commitment, perseverance, and a firm conviction that one's career pursuits can bring honour to God.

As more individuals respond to their God-given call to faith-based entrepreneurship, a modest but significant shift is occurring inside the business world. This shift views business as an opportunity to significantly contribute to one's business or a faith-driven entrepreneur group, as an extension of one's faith and a mission to serve. It also views business as a method of survival and wealth accumulation.

The guiding precepts of Islam establish the rules that govern every facet of economic dealings in the Muslim world. The influence of faith and religious convictions on moral business conduct is significant.

To understand the phrase "faith-based entrepreneurship," we must first distinguish between the concepts of "faith-based" and "entrepreneurship." An entrepreneur can be defined as a person who starts and runs a business and continues to do so because of the drive to create and function autonomously. Having an affiliation with religion is a prerequisite for being a person of faith. By combining the two classifications, we can characterise a firm with a religious affiliation as faith-based entrepreneurship.

Fundamentally, faith-based entrepreneurship is about realising that business is the opportunity to do more for society than turn a profit. Entrepreneurs who adopt this strategy usually aim to use their connections, abilities, and resources to leverage their religious convictions to positively impact their local communities and society as a whole. They see their endeavours as means of influencing the world in line with their religious beliefs, emulating morals, and disseminating a message.

Muslim business owners are advised to exercise caution when conducting business and building connections with people. Some of these cautions include acting in good faith, upholding the truth, refraining from lying, and refraining from taking needless oaths when speaking.

Although a Muslim entrepreneur can choose, religious values guide how that freedom should be used. Merely adhering to the five pillars of Islam is insufficient; they must also run their businesses with faith (iman), which translates into obeying the law (Syariah), doing what is allowed (halal), and abstaining from what is prohibited (haram).

One of the fundamental components of Islamic business ethics is that entrepreneurs have true intention in all their dealings. True intention establishes an objective or goal in the infusion of the heart; it is the foundation of an act in Islam. Sincere intention and good faith are typically accompanied by Allah's selected course of action – to establish a productive and profitable business, an entrepreneur needs to be truthful, have good intentions, and act in good faith.

Therefore, Muslims must discern between what is haram or immoral and what is halal or moral. They must also distinguish between good and bad intentions and right versus wrong, fair versus unfair, and just versus unjust.

> *The Almighty Allah says: "Surely we have revealed to you the Book with the truth, therefore serve Allah, being sincere to Him in obedience" (Quran, 39:2)*

In light of the foregoing, a Muslim business owner should ensure that their true intentions in all dealings are to further virtuous causes and win the pleasure of Allah in all spheres of life by sincerity and good faith.

> *"O you who believe... Be not unfaithful to Allah and the Apostle, nor be unfaithful to your trusts while you know" (Qur'an; 8:27)*

The verse affirms that all business decisions and actions are predicated on the principles of faith and equal treatment.

Faith-based enterprise has unique challenges and exciting opportunities in an ever-evolving global market. In the face of rising secularism and shifting cultural norms, faith-based entrepreneurs must carefully combine their religious convictions with the demands of a market fuelled by innovation and profit.

Faith-based entrepreneurship combines economic and religious ideas to establish a company with a strong religious foundation. This innovative business method integrates spiritual principles while aiming to strike a balance between monetary objectives and moral and ethical standards. Recently, there has been a surge in the popularity of faith-based entrepreneurship as Islamic company owners seek to incorporate their religious convictions into their ventures.

Relationship between Faith and Business Success

Islam states that business owners and entrepreneurs must have Taqwa (faith) in Allah Almighty. This implies that for them to succeed, faith in Allah SWT and his Messenger, Muhammad SAW, is a must.

> *In Quran Allah says, "O you who have believed, shall I guide you to a transaction that will save you from a painful punishment? [It is that] you believe in Allah and His Messenger and strive in the cause of Allah with your wealth and your lives. That is best for you, if you should know." (Quran 61:10-11)*

An entrepreneur who achieves both Taqwa of Allah and Iman greatness through profitable ventures is considered successful.

The foundation of Islam is good faith, which also serves as the motivation for a believer's deeds. A person who strives to be the best version of themselves in their relationships with God and others is in a state of attentiveness and awareness of God in all facets of life.

However, the notion of good faith, often referred to in Islam as Ihsan, is a crucial component of the religion that impacts people's lives and the well-being of society. The pinnacle of faith, Ihsan, is reached when a person aspires to perfection in their interactions with God and other people.

> *Prophet Muhammad (PBUH) said, "Ihsan is to worship Allah as if you see Him, and if you do not see Him, then indeed He sees you." (Sahih Muslim)*

This hadith emphasises the need to strive for excellence in our deeds and be aware of God's presence in our lives, knowing He is constantly observing and knowledgeable of our intentions. It is often known that highly religious people are also the most successful people. The most common association of faith seems to be with religion. As a result, there is ultimately less conversation regarding faith in a secular context. This is unfortunate, as faith is a wonderful word that conveys a potent idea.

Nobody who lacks trust in themselves or others has ever taken the risk to launch a new company, go on an adventure, pick up a new skill, accept a physical challenge, get married, or try to change another person's life. Faith in our own talents as well as others' abilities is necessary for all of these deeds.

In sum, faith can play a noteworthy role in any enterprise's success. Remember that it may manifest in various forms and affect individuals and organisations differently. Faith can significantly impact business prosperity by providing ethical regulation, nurturing resilience, offering community support and much more.

How do Islamic values influence entrepreneurial mindset and decision-making?

As an entrepreneur, attitude is what drives one's and ultimately manifests in success. To guarantee a company's success, entrepreneurs must clearly outline their objectives and long-term plans, which can only be done with sufficient psychological preparation for entrepreneurship.

It is evident that Islamic values greatly influence Muslim entrepreneurs. Establishing a framework based on moral and ethical principles from the Quran and Hadith can also mould Muslim entrepreneurs' entrepreneurial mindsets and decision-making processes.

These principles encourage moral behaviour, the importance of accountability, and communal welfare, which impacts how Muslim business owners handle their enterprises. Let us examine how these values affect an entrepreneurial attitude and decision-making process.

"A mental attitude or inclination" is the literal definition of mentality. A mindset is a collection of ideas and responses that combine to form the totality rather than just one feature. The "entrepreneurial mindset" is a reflection of profound cognitive phenomena, including profound assumptions and religious convictions.

In the case of Muslim entrepreneurs, these could be the idealised forms of Islamic business and beliefs. Muslim business owners are concerned with orienting their perspectives within the framework of Al-Sharia, the Islamic legal code, to take advantage of any prospective halal prospects.

Islamic values significantly shape entrepreneurial mindset and decision-making through principles like honesty, social responsibility, and fairness. Entrepreneurs are guided by ethical conduct (Sidq and Amanah), social welfare (Zakat), and justice (Adl). Prohibition of usury (Riba) leads to profit-sharing models, while stewardship (Khalifah) encourages sustainability.

Moderation (Israf) promotes resource management, and respect for human dignity (Karamah) ensures fair treatment of employees and customers. Innovation within Islamic guidelines (Ijtihad) is also valued. These principles create businesses that balance financial success with ethical conduct, social responsibility, and sustainability, aligning with broader spiritual and moral objectives.

Role of spirituality in cultivating resilience and purpose in business

An essential component of Islamic entrepreneurship is spirituality. Islam and spirituality are strongly intertwined since Islam holds that the only reason for being a Muslim is to serve Allah SWT, as humankind was created with this intention. Muslims are encouraged by Islam to live flawless lives as Allah's servants. Regular worships provide the added benefit of improving the servant's living environment.

Because faith in Allah SWT permeates every part of life, Islam does not draw a line between the material and spiritual realms. The economic theory guiding business towards Rabbani, or God-oriented principles, drives Islamic entrepreneurship, influencing spirituality in the field.

> *"And those who strive for Us - We will surely guide them to Our ways. And indeed, Allah is with the doers of good"* (Quran, 29:69)

Muslim entrepreneurship strongly emphasises integrating spiritual and material aspects of life since Islam ideally functions in all spheres of life to perform its role as the world's Khalifa. Therefore, Muslim business owners should consider the spiritual elements that underpin their purpose for doing business and view it from a materialistic standpoint.

> *"Thus when they fulfil their term appointed, either take them back on equitable terms; and take for witness two persons from among you, endued with justice, and establish the evidence for the sake of God. Such is the admonition given to him who believes in God and the Last Day. And for those who fear God, He (ever) prepares a way out. And He provides for him from (sources) he never could expect. And if anyone puts his trust in God, sufficient is (God) for him. For God will surely accomplish His purpose: verily, for all things has God appointed a due proportion"* (Quran, 65:2-3)

These verses elucidate the importance of true piety in alignment with Allah SWT's will and plan. Islam views piety as a source of inspiration and defines motivation as the will spurred on by God's will, motivated by the strength of trust towards Allah SWT's aid in all facets of life, including business. Islam strongly focuses on even quality and outstanding performance in all economic undertakings through a hadith that al-Bayhaqi recounts.

> *"Surely Allah loves a person when he does a job, he does it with earnestness" (Hadith, Al-Bayhaqi)*

Spirituality creates positive attitudes and behaviours. It is strongly linked to internal factors based on belief towards Allah SWT and is applied in entrepreneurship. Themes and subthemes pertaining to the traits of spiritual practices motivate entrepreneurs to develop their self-assurance and tenacity, maintain moral principles, and support responsible management, all of which will contribute to their success in their efforts.

Spirituality is crucial for promoting resilience and purpose in the workplace because it provides a deeper sense of meaning and purpose. In addition to supporting entrepreneurial efforts, applying psychological resilience and optimism favourably correlates with entrepreneurial performance. Without a doubt, optimism boosts motivation and goal orientation, and psychological resilience enables people to create backup plans for goals and deal with the challenges of starting their own businesses.

Gaining the desired success in business can be attained through deepening one's spirituality, self-awareness, and perseverance in trying circumstances. Resilience is, therefore, a skill that businesses need to possess.

An entrepreneur's resilience refers to their ability to handle challenging situations, adjust, and bounce back from adversity based on personal resources and interactions with their surroundings. Resilient entrepreneurs are those who can grow and mobilise their resources in the face of adversity. They perceive obstacles and failures as chances for development and education, embracing change as a necessary aspect of life and an opportunity to grow and adapt rather than fighting it. They possess confidence in their ability to navigate uncertainty and overcome challenges with grace and resiliency.

Adopting a spiritual outlook can help entrepreneurs weather the ups and downs of the entrepreneurial path with composure and grit despite its inherent challenges and unpredictability.

Success in entrepreneurship can be greatly impacted by embracing spirituality on a personal and professional level. Entrepreneurs may tap into a deeper reservoir of inspiration, resiliency, and creativity by developing mindfulness and appreciation, aligning with a sense of purpose, and trusting their intuition.

Thus, by adopting a spiritual outlook, business owners can develop a stronger sense of purpose, connect with their inner selves, and discover the inspiration and fortitude required to overcome obstacles and realise their objectives.

Entrepreneurs who develop their spiritual resilience can reap several advantages that improve their effectiveness and well-being:

Greater Spirit of Purpose and Fulfilment: By aligning with their core values and a sense of purpose, entrepreneurs may discover meaning and fulfilment in their businesses. This heightened sense of purpose fuels motivation and satisfaction.

Improved Problem-Solving Skills: Spiritually resilient businesspeople are more equipped to handle obstacles with inventiveness, adaptability, and resilience by drawing on their inner strength and perspective.

Enhanced mental agility: Spiritual resilience produces increased self-awareness and sensitivity, which empowers business owners to handle interpersonal relationships with empathy, understanding, and compassion.

Better Stress Management: Entrepreneurs who possess spiritual resilience can handle stress and lessen the detrimental effects that work-related pressures have on their physical and mental well-being.

Thus, entrepreneurs can overcome hardship with generosity, resilience, and effectiveness by cultivating a sense of power within, connection, and purpose. Establishing a purpose-driven company that integrates commercial objectives with spiritual values enables them to not only make a profit but also positively impact society and the well-being of everyone involved.

Chapter Two

Faith-Based Leadership and Vision

Islam offers laws for worldly and spiritual things, including how businesses should be conducted. One of the pillars of our social activities is leadership – a procedure for motivating and encouraging people to work arduously towards a goal. Leadership is crucial to success, whether a business is formal or informal, small or large.

According to Islam, a leader guides a group that is supposed to use influence to establish and achieve moral aims and objectives. Building a team and fostering a sense of unity is essential to a leader's success.

> *A person is encouraged to develop good behaviours and characteristics (Al-Bukhari)*

This suggests that a leader should exhibit a well-balanced demeanour – assertive yet nonviolent, giving yet not showy, and forgiving yet not cowardly.

> *According to the Prophet (PBUH), "Every one of you is a shepherd and every shepherd has accountability for his*

flock," everyone in Islam has some degree of leadership responsibility (Sahih Muslim)

Integrating Faith into Leadership and Visionary Thinking

Muslims believe that Islamic principles apply to everyone. Thus, trust is the foundation of Islamic leadership. It stands for a moral and religious pledge made by leaders to their adherents that they will do everything in their power to defend, mentor, and treat them fairly. Islamic leadership centres on performing good deeds for the benefit of humanity, the Muslim community, and Allah. It facilitates a person's pursuit of happiness in both realms.

The term "dependence on Allah" (Tawakkul) refers to total trust and confidence in the Almighty Allah. Every action, desire, plan, policy, and method used to accomplish the objectives must adhere to Islamic principles. An Islamic leader must rely on Allah to see these objectives through to completion since Tawakkul uplifts the leader and assists in making wise judgements.

Moreover, faith-based leadership in Islamic entrepreneurship integrates ethical principles, ensuring Shariah compliance and prioritising social responsibility. It promotes a long-term vision rooted in stewardship and encourages community collaboration and servant leadership.

As said by Allah in the Holy Quran:

> *"And will provide for him from where he does not expect. And whoever places his trust in Allah, Sufficient is He for him, for Allah will surely accomplish His Purpose: For verily, Allah has appointed for all things a due proportion" (Quran, 65:3)*

The Quran above says to always have faith and confidence in Allah. Our challenging moments can only be supported and guided by Allah. The Holy Quran shows that Tawakkul is a need rather than an option, as stated by Allah Almighty. Entrepreneurs are spiritually motivated, viewing their work as worship and striving for economic justice and equity.

Integrating faith into leadership and visionary thinking in Islam is essentially a process of following Islamic values in business as an entrepreneur. The following are the important aspects to consider while doing so:

- Islamic leadership embraces a vision that directs motivation to work for the betterment of others, i.e., society, and regulates it according to stewardship principles (Khalifah).

- The Islamic ethic of Sidq (truthfulness) and Amanah (trustworthiness) ensures that ethical conduct is based on honesty and respect, thereby creating a culture of respect.

- Islamic leadership must integrate Adl (justice) to ensure everyone is treated fairly and equally.

- Islamic leaders must promote the participation of all business members in affairs to ensure cohesiveness and consider diverse viewpoints.

- Knowledge sustains hope and fortification, enabling leaders to persevere with Sabr and to rely on Tawakkul in the face of adversity. This spiritual grounding applies tenacity and flexibility in the face of adversity.

- Islamic leadership fosters a compassionate culture that cares for its people and ensures an optimal working atmosphere.

Thus, Islamic leaders may apply all these faith-based principles to build a visionary and ethical business model that achieves both spiritual and organisational success and solidity.

Applying Islamic teachings to set visionary goals as business entrepreneurs

A visionary leader can favourably administrate true and effective attributes that contribute to social progress. Islam, a religion advocating harmony and peace, guides us as Muslim entrepreneurs towards the right path by enlightening spirituality and helping us understand the state of the world. It provides laws, moral principles, and guidelines of conduct that enable us to comprehend our religion and live our lives in accordance with Shariah. It is with these resources that we develop the genuine qualities of leadership.

As Muslim entrepreneurs, our lives should involve careful planning in moral, political, social, and commercial endeavours. The Quran teaches Muslim business owners to be planners and strategists, illustrating this through accounts of the prophets, the natural law of Allah (SWT), and the praise of those with insight and foresight. Our plans must not be narrow-minded but encompass both immediate and long-term concerns relevant to the objective.

Moreover, we must not allow little things to derail us from achieving our goals. The capacity to look beyond one's immediate surroundings and circumstances is known as vision. If a plan is created without vision and understanding, it might or might not be as effective. Those of us who possess vision are praised by Allah (SWT). The Islamic Sunnah includes goal-setting, planning, and developing tactics to meet objectives in line with the teachings of the Quran and Prophet Muhammad (PBUH).

Applying Islamic teachings to setting visionary goals for business entails incorporating key aspects of the Quran and Hadith into the overall planning and goal formulation process. Here are some ways we can achieve this:

Ethical Integrity and Trustworthiness

Goal: Uphold high standards of integrity and credibility in all aspects of business.

Application: Pay attention to business integrity, customer and employee relations and compliance with ethical standards. Develop and enforce measures that ensure accountability and foster stakeholder confidence.

Innovation and Continuous Improvement

Goal: Foster innovation and continuous improvement.

Application: Encourage freedom of thought and creativity while adhering to the norms of Islamic Shariah. Research to increase the quality of both products and services. Cultivate an organisational learning environment and organisational flexibility to gain competitive advantages.

Balanced Profit and Purpose

Goal: Combine economic rationality with ethical and religious motives.

Application: Set realistic targets that prioritise ethical considerations alongside financial goals. Stress the creation and accumulation of long-term value while ignoring the short-term outcomes or consequences. Ensure that business success benefits not only the company but also the wider community.

Compassionate Leadership

Goal: Be sensitive to employees' feelings and needs.

Application: Follow the path set by the Prophet Muhammad (PBUH) to lead with compassion (Rahmah) and empathy. First, focus on caring for employees, fostering a healthy organisational climate, and responding to their issues honestly.

When applied to strategic business planning, these Islamic teachings ensure that the goals to be achieved provide for material and spiritual well-being and social justice. This integrated approach pays attention to the fact that business organisations should be socially responsible and align with the tenets of Islamic Shariah.

The Role of Trust in Divine Guidance (Tawakkul)

The four fundamental tenets of Islamic business – accountability, freedom, justice (balancing), and Monotheism – provide the framework for ethical entrepreneurship.

As entrepreneurs, we should possess the following five interior qualities: Wara' (fear of being forever hidden from God), Tawakkul (confidence in Allah /total surrender to His will), Zuhd (detachment of materialism), Shukr (thankfulness), Sabr (patience/steadfastness), and Wara' (fear of being an eternal stranger). Understanding fair income thresholds and avoiding jealousy towards successful businesses and forbidden business activities are marks of responsible entrepreneurship.

Let us never forget that the secret to having a happy view of life and business is Tawakkul. Within Islamic thinking, Tawakkul—an Arabic term loosely translates to "reliance" or "trust in God"—is a profound idea. It represents a well-rounded way of living in which self-reliance and faith in a higher force coexist harmoniously. This idea may be applied outside religious settings and is a powerful mental model for dealing with uncertainty in both life and business.

> *"Say, 'never will we be struck except by what Allah has decreed for us; He is our protector.' And upon Allah let the believers rely." (Quran, 9:51)*

This verse highlights the importance of trusting in Allah's decree while taking action to pursue our goals, a crucial mindset in entrepreneurship.

As Muslims, we are encouraged not to feel helpless and fatalistic, even as we place our reliance on Allah (SWT). Alongside teaching acceptance of fate, Islam also provides guidance on minimising the likelihood of misfortunes and losses. It's important to note that risk management is consistent with the idea of Tawakkul, or faith in Allah. We should first employ the most suitable means of accomplishing our objectives and then place our trust in Allah for a better outcome.

> *"And whoever relies upon Allah, and then He is sufficient for him. Indeed, Allah will accomplish His purpose. Allah has already set for everything a (decreed) extent" (Qur'an; 65:3)*

In a hadith from Sunan Tirmidhi, a conversation between a man and Prophet Muhammad (PBUH) encapsulates exactly what God has done and what humanity has done. The man, preparing for a journey, has not yet tied his camel.

> *When the Prophet Muhammad (PBUH) asks the man why the camel is untied, the man responds, "I put my trust in Allah." The Prophet Muhammad (PBUH) then replied, "Tie your camel first and then put your trust in Allah" (Tirmidhi)*

We must take a step back from our work, reflect on Allah, and tell ourselves, "Ya Allah, I embrace this path that you have carved out for me. I am aware that my path is unique from everyone else's. I am aware that it might have taken this individual a year to accumulate a million dollars, but my goodness, I do not care if it takes me five or ten. Whatever path you have planned for me, I believe in it. I am confident that it will materialise. I will gladly follow whatever route you have planned for me and overcome any challenges you may have put in my way to teach me lessons. I will also take pleasure in the entire experience." We need to be upbeat and full of faith in Allah.

Dependency must be moderated and balanced. As entrepreneurs, we must use our God-given abilities—both physical and mental—to the fullest extent possible to succeed in our endeavours. To do this, we must educate ourselves in finance, marketing, and business. We must constantly pray to God (Allah) in response to this; we cannot just remain at home and hope for a miracle to solve our problems. However, as God is the source of sustenance, He must also be considered. In other words, we have to put in the work, but He gets the reward.

To stop being so critical of ourselves for not reaching certain salary levels, ambitions, or milestones, we need to master Tawakkul. We can find joy in entrepreneurship by surrendering control with a positive outlook and depending exclusively on Allah. It should not be something we fear or feel is holding us down. For a significant portion of our journey, we might have struggled to balance embracing and letting go, driven by our inner urge to consistently reach milestones.

It was not until we began to practice Tawakkul – placing our trust in Allah – that we began to feel better in our daily lives. As we learned to truly rely on Allah, we moved from a scarcity mindset to one of abundance.

Prophetic Examples of Visionary Leadership

What sort of leadership do we wish to see in the modern world? And why do so many leaders not live up to our standards?

More and more concerns are being raised about persons in positions of authority as we experience the global fallout from bad leadership. Whether one looks in the "East" or the "West," it is evident that we live in a period when the global community demands better leadership. The media and society at large make plain the general public's discontent with corrupt and unfair leadership and the erosion of confidence in numerous leaders and institutions.

According to Michael Hart's book "The 100: A Ranking of the Best Influential People in History," Prophet Muhammad (PBUH) was "the only man [we can say leader] in the past who was extraordinarily successful on both the worldly and religious level." The Prophet (PBUH) was chosen by Allah Almighty to serve as the representative of the Muslims in Madina and the entire Muslim Ummah.

> *In Surah Al-Anbiya, Allah says: 'We appointed them as leaders to guide by our command, and we revealed to them the doing of good, the establishment of prayer, and the giving of zakah. They were devoted worshipers of us alone' (Quran 21:73)*

And we all know that His decision was remarkable. The Prophet Muhammad's leadership has greatly influenced the way that leadership is perceived and applied both inside and outside of the Muslim community. He is frequently held up as an example of perfect governance in Islamic history.

In addition to being acknowledged as the last prophet of Islam, he was also a statesman, an army officer, a community activist, and a spiritual leader. According to the Law of Navigation, a leader must establish his people's direction and guide them there. The Prophet consistently maintained the larger picture for the Muslims at the forefront of his own and their thoughts. He never lost sight of the bigger goal and the final reward.

People are still motivated to be better leaders by the exceptional leadership of the Prophet Muhammad. His example shows us that great leadership is about service, compassion, and a commitment to the greater good rather than authority or power.

Effective leadership requires integrity, empathy, vision, planning, and ecumenical interaction. We can learn from his role model and seek direction from his teachings to build a more equitable, peaceful, and wealthy society as we work to become more effective managers in our respective industries.

Allah describes leadership in the Quran as:

> *"Indeed, Allah commands you to render trust to whom they are due and when you judge between people to judge with justice. Excellent is that which Allah instructs you. Indeed, Allah is ever Hearing and seeing." (Quran 4:58)*

Let us now examine some significant facets of Prophet Muhammad's governance:

Set a Good Example: Prophet Muhammad always exhibited the moral principles and conduct he taught. His integrity, humility, compassion, and honesty made him an exemplary figure for those who followed him.

Humility: Prophet Muhammad maintained his approachability and humility in spite of his position of leadership. He was well-known for interacting with individuals from all walks of life and assisting with small jobs.

His inclusive leadership brought many tribes and groups together under the Islamic flag. He emphasised that all believers are equal, regardless of their origin.

Empathy & Compassion: He exhibited great empathy and compassion for everyone, regardless of social or economic standing. He was kind to the downtrodden and frequently went above and beyond to assist people in need.

Conflict Resolution: Whenever feasible, the Prophet Muhammad gave priority to resolving disputes amicably. He promoted forgiveness and reconciliation, strengthening the community's sense of cohesion.

Justice and Fairness: Prophet Muhammad was devoted to upholding justice and fairness, ensuring that even those who opposed him received fair treatment. He underlined the crucial importance of protecting rights and abstaining from oppression.

Consultation in Decision-Making: Prophet Muhammad respected the advice of his companions and asked them to speak with him on significant issues. He made decisions by shura, or consultation, exhibiting humility and regard for the opinions of others.

Courage and Resilience: Through his leadership, he showed courage and resilience in times of adversity. He persevered in the face of persecution, hostility, and even assassination attempts.

Communication Skills: He had a strong ability to communicate and persuade others with his message. People from various backgrounds could relate to and easily understand his sermons and teachings.

Long-Term Vision: He had an all-encompassing plan for civilisation that included social, spiritual, and economic aspects. His teachings offered principles for social organisation and human behaviour.

Flexibility: He modified his leadership style according to the situation and requirements of his neighbourhood. As the group flourished, his leadership style changed from spiritual direction to military and administrative command.

Prophet Muhammad's leadership is frequently viewed as a comprehensive model that tackles a variety of leadership facets, such as ethical standards, strategic thinking, developing a sense of community, and personal character. Regardless of their religious beliefs, world leaders are still motivated by his example to aspire to be compassionate, just, and humble in their work as leaders.

Lessons from Prophet Muhammad's strategic vision in business and community development

In the nearly 2,500 years of documented history, the world has witnessed many exceptional strategists. The Prophet of Islam, however, employed a fairly broad range of tactics. The Prophet's sphere of influence was vast.

All facets of human existence—personal, religious, social, philosophical, spiritual, diplomatic, political, commercial, and administrative—have been profoundly impacted by his influence. No other strategist in recorded history has had such a profound and wide-ranging impact on the entirety of human existence.

"A plan, method or series of manoeuvres or stratagems for obtaining a particular objective or result" is the definition of strategy. A plan or strategy developed or employed to achieve an objective or to obtain an edge over an opponent is known as a stratagem.

Prophet Muhammad (PBUH) was a skilled tactician who could thoroughly assess a situation and devise workable solutions. Though he would confer and solicit advice from his friends, he would always base his ultimate decision on his own discernment and Allah's instructions. His military conquests, his talks with other tribes, and his administration of the affairs of the fledgling Islamic state were all clear examples of his strategic decision-making and thinking abilities.

Prophet Muhammad's leadership style also included a visionary approach, which was crucial. He was quite clear about what he intended to do and went after it with great vigour. His worldview included the social, political, and economic facets of society in addition to the spiritual world.

In his ideal society, where everyone would have the chance to prosper and advance the common good, there would be justice, equality, and brotherhood. He put in a lot of effort to create such a society, and people are still motivated by his vision today.

Prophet Muhammad exercised leadership not only within his own community but also in his dealings with other communities. He addressed followers of various faiths with dignity and respect, setting an example for interfaith cooperation and communication.

He would respect their freedom to practise their religion while extending an invitation to Islam. His pioneering and avant-garde leadership in this area continues to motivate others to strive for improved interfaith harmony and intercultural understanding.

The epitome of genuine leadership lies in the Holy Prophet Muhammad (PBUH), who possessed traits that we can apply to our own lives – both private and public – to realise the full potential of each and every one of life's domains. By embracing sincerity, passion, and inspiration, we pave the path towards becoming effective leaders, gaining the great qualities of a true leader.

> *"There has certainly been for you in the Messenger of Allah an excellent pattern for anyone whose hope is in Allah and the Last Day and [who] remembers Allah often" (Quran 33:21)*

How does faith-based leadership inspire innovation and creativity?

In the hectic business world, we hear a lot about innovation, but we hardly ever connect it with our faith. Is it feasible that your faith may be the key ingredient that ignites your leadership creativity and innovation?

Innovation in the secular world is frequently driven by trends, market competitiveness, and financial results. But what if we adopted an alternative strategy? As Muslims, we have the chance to let our creativity be inspired by our faith, making our work a means of glorifying God.

Belief empowers us to see beyond the commonplace and venture into uncharted territory. It gives us the bravery to think creatively and beyond the box, take calculated chances and create with an ulterior motive. When your work transforms into a canvas for creativity, it transcends mere routine and becomes more than "just a job".

We can overcome the paralysing fear of failing by placing our faith in God. We realise that God's grand design for us may include even our mistakes. Because we know that God is directing our actions, this trust gives us the confidence to be daring and creative.

The ideas of ijtihad, or critical legal thought in pursuit of solutions to novel situations, and bidah, or innovation, are two of the most significant aspects of Islam that make it a mobile notion. Islam has significant historical mobility because of its close adherence to bidah and ijtihad, which allows it to maintain continuity with the past while reviving its life as a dynamic faith.

Faith-based leadership defines purpose, motivates change, encourages imagination driven by values, and ensures integrity, strength, diversity, creativity, teamwork, and mission. Incorporating all these elements, faith-based leaders develop contexts that foster innovation to solve critical problems and enhance lives.

Chapter Three

Entrepreneurial Resilience and Perseverance

Persevering and persisting through difficulties to achieve a higher goal is commendable. It is a quality we should all cultivate. No one disagrees that resilience is an essential characteristic to possess. Adapting and recovering from challenges and adversity is a vital skill that every individual needs to develop to thrive in life. Islam provides a unique perspective on resilience, emphasising the importance of trust in Allah, patience, and perseverance in facing life's challenges. Islam greatly emphasises preparedness, resilience, and taking practical measures when needed.

> Allah says, "And take provisions, but indeed, the best provision is Taqwa (piety). So fear Me, O people of understanding." (Quran 2:197)

This verse emphasises the need for preparedness and that true protection comes from a strong connection with Allah.

Business resilience is essential to starting, running, and growing enterprises. The term "business resilience" describes an organisation's or firm's capacity to adapt, adjust, and change its business plans. Businesses' ability to predict an unexpected business environment is implied by their business resilience.

Resilience is what enables firms to survive setbacks and interruptions and carry on with operations—or, more crucially, to prosper. For entrepreneurs, resilience is a true strategy for business growth. If resilience is considered a critical factor in determining an entrepreneur's capacity to continue the business venture, then entrepreneurs with higher degrees of resilience are also expected to have more successful businesses.

It makes sense to believe that resilience contributes to the success of entrepreneurship. In entrepreneurship, resilience is the ability to overcome obstacles in high-stakes business situations and continue with business operations in the face of unanticipated events and challenging circumstances. Entrepreneurship is risky; one can only expect it to be with its stumbling blocks. But these are barriers that faith-based resilience can be employed to overcome, so let's see how.

Building Resilience Through Faith

As Muslims, faith empowers us to become more resilient by offering a bigger picture of our current situation. It lifts our spirits, shielding us from depression during challenging times. Faith forces us to see the world from a different viewpoint, one that is frequently based on hope and a catalyst for a transformative outlook. Those who subscribe to the notion that there is a long-term plan for kindness and hope are considered to be people of faith.

In Islam, we are urged to hold fast to our beliefs and trust in Allah's omniscience. Such thinking assists us in reframing failures as chances for personal development, leading to increased mental toughness.

Both the Quran and Hadith underscore the importance of patience and endurance in navigating life's trails.

> *Allah assures us in the Quran that with hardship comes ease. "For indeed, with hardship [will be] ease. Indeed, with hardship [will be] ease." (Quran 94:5-6)*

Through his suffering and persecution in promoting Islam, the Prophet (SAW) demonstrated extraordinary patience. Despite losing loved ones, including his uncle Abu Talib and his wife Khadija (RA), he persisted with a strong sense of resolve. He was thrown out of Mecca, beaten, laughed at, and derided, yet he replied with courage, discernment, and integrity. Resilience gives us the energy to recover over time, while perseverance helps us get by in the here and now.

Islam's Taqwa and resilience develop invincible psychological strength. Maintaining mental resilience in a time of uncertainty, stress, and misfortune is more important than ever. Islam provides invaluable ideas and customs that support this enduring power.

At the core of Islam lies the concept of Taqwa, translated as "piety" or "God-consciousness". It highlights the awareness of God in all facets of life, guiding individuals towards virtuous deeds and beliefs.

Perseverance is further facilitated by resilience, enabling individuals to press forward in their endeavours despite significant challenges. This attribute is consistent with the idea of Tawakkul, which is closely associated with *Taqwa* and refers to dependence on God.

Through the integration of faith-based values and the ability to adjust, surmount, and endure, we entrepreneurs can skillfully and resolutely handle life's obstacles. This powerful connection is an invitation to study Islamic teachings and principles and a route to increased psychological fortitude.

Moreover, the notion of perseverance in Islam encompasses proactive measures to confront obstacles and triumph over misfortune. As Muslims, we are encouraged to put our faith in Allah and work hard to better our circumstances.

> *The Quran states, "Indeed, Allah will not change the condition of a people until they change what is in themselves" (Quran 13:11)*

This verse highlights the significance of acting to improve things while acknowledging Allah's supreme sovereignty.

Overcoming challenges and setbacks with faith-based resilience

Faith-based resilience offers us an entirely different perspective that instils hope and strength as entrepreneurs. Relying on our faith and religious beliefs, we recognise the transient nature of challenges, striving instead for the greater good. In the realm of faith-based resilience, setbacks are viewed not as failures but as learning opportunities.

Within Islam, entrepreneurs possess a strength beyond the confines of commerce because of our unshakable bond with God. Our faith in a personally involved God guides us as we seek prosperity. Our strong religious convictions shape our outlook, granting us tenacity and purpose and fueling our desire to invent and create.

Religion is integral to the business ventures of deeply religious entrepreneurs. Because religious convictions can spur creative entrepreneurship, innovation and faith go hand in hand. Trusting in a personally involved God provides direction and encouragement in our entrepreneurial endeavours. We take chances and make critical decisions based on this belief. Faith grants us the grit and tenacity to pursue our dreams.

Our faith in a responsive God equips us with the strength to deal with the unpredictability of entrepreneurship. Faith serves as a compass, helping us maintain focus on our goals and inspiring us to take calculated risks in pursuit of success.

> *"And whoever fears Allah – He will make for him a way out and will provide for him from where he does not expect. And whoever relies upon Allah – then He is sufficient for him." (Quran 65:2-3)*

As spiritual entrepreneurs, we need to constantly hone our adaptability and resilience skills and learn to see setbacks as chances for personal development. The world of faith-based entrepreneurship can be both gratifying and difficult to navigate, and development and success are frequently accompanied by various challenges and failures. With the correct tactics and attitude, we can overcome these difficulties and come out on the other side stronger, wiser, and in a better position to carry out our goal and vision.

> *The Prophet Muhammad (PBUH) said: "Strive for that which will benefit you, seek the help of Allah, and do not feel helpless." (Sahih Muslim)*

Faith as a source of resilience for entrepreneurs

When conquering challenges in your entrepreneurial journey, faith may be a very useful tool. A spiritual practice and philosophy can guide you through adversity with bravery, discernment, and honesty. To overcome obstacles in your faith-based business, consider the following strategies:

Think about Your Spiritual Core Ideals: Let your spiritual ideals direct your choices. When confronting and overcoming obstacles in your business, consider how these principles might guide your decisions and actions.

Pray for Wisdom & Guidance: Seek wisdom and guidance from prayer during difficult times. Seek guidance and inspiration from God to aid you in your faith-based business journey by making wise decisions and overcoming challenges.

Share Your Journey With Like-Minded Entrepreneurs: Make connections with other entrepreneurs who are driven by faith and exchange your experiences, struggles, and victories. This sense of belonging can offer a forum for growth, encouragement, and mutual learning.

Entrepreneurs who anchor their faith in God are able to persevere despite adversity and carry on with their entrepreneurial endeavours. Faith serves as a compass, helping business owners stay aligned with their goals and encouraging them to venture into calculated risks for success. Moreover, faith shapes an entrepreneur's perspective because it gives them the conviction that their work is a divine calling and that a higher power is behind them.

> *"And seek help through patience and prayer, and indeed, it is difficult except for the humbly submissive [to Allah]." (Quran 2:45)*

This verse highlights the importance of patience and prayer as sources of strength and guidance during difficult times, encouraging entrepreneurs to rely on their faith for resilience.

Strategies for maintaining perseverance and determination in entrepreneurship

Characteristics like perseverance and tenacity are crucial for economic success, personal development, and general well-being. These characteristics can help entrepreneurs like yourself to overcome obstacles, accomplish objectives, and deal with challenging circumstances. Let us face it: almost every entrepreneur will encounter setbacks or failures at some point, making perseverance an essential quality.

Mistakes are inevitable; they are part of the learning process. As reiterated several times before, we are all going to make mistakes in life. However, the most crucial trait an entrepreneur can possess is the ability to bounce back after falling on hard times and learn from mistakes. Perseverance, therefore, becomes necessary.

> *Allah states that "only those who practice patience and self-restraint will be granted such goodness, and these are the ones who are truly fortunate" (Quran 41:35)*

Thus, to be a tenacious and committed entrepreneur, consider these three essential strategies:

Stay committed to your goals.

Setting and achieving company objectives is rarely simple. Most entrepreneurs see attaining their objectives and dreams as their primary mission, but if one does not persevere, it is simple for them to give up. It takes time for dreams to come true, and simply dreaming is not enough to make them come true.

To turn your dreams into reality, you must maintain your attention and never stop working towards your goals. Having a clear understanding of your objectives and focusing on the finish line is the first step in remaining persistent. Every entrepreneur striving for success needs to keep in mind why they are working so hard. Anybody with a goal understands that the payoff is worthwhile.

Organise your goals and objectives.

The capacity to divide your overarching objective into smaller, more doable activities is a critical component of success. Smaller goals will help you accomplish your objectives more quickly and also provide a motivational boost, which is exactly what an entrepreneur needs while they are attempting to persevere.

Your plans can become overly ambitious, and no matter what you do, you might never feel as though you are making progress towards an unrealistic objective. When you set ambitious goals, you may feel overwhelmed. However, by breaking your goals down, you can concentrate on one more manageable activity at a time, which increases the efficiency and effectiveness of reaching your goal.

Envision yourself succeeding.

The path to success is never simple, regardless of whether you are just starting out or are an experienced entrepreneur. But difficult does not equate to unachievable. If you can maintain your perseverance and keep your final objective in mind, you can succeed in business. Failure does not guarantee success; your determination can overcome any obstacles in your path. Visualising success is critical in this journey.

Like life itself, the life of your business is frequently played out in stages: you try, you fail, you try again, and maybe you get lucky, but it is not always easy sailing. Being persistent requires optimism as well because it is only when you have faith in your ability to attain your ultimate objective that you will succeed. The source of perseverance is inside; it involves identifying your drive and using it for both your company and yourself.

As business owners, we can control our own fate and realise our dreams. But our tenacity is what gives this power its fuel. In the midst of difficulty, let's not forget that what will ultimately determine our success is our unshakable dedication to our objectives, our fortitude in the face of failures, and our determination to keep going.

Learning from Adversity: Examples of Resilient Entrepreneurs

Entrepreneurship is not easy and is filled with risks and failures, yet it is in overcoming these adversities that some of the greatest stories of success emerge. In this section of the book, you will find inspiration in the accounts of Muslim entrepreneurs who have faced hardships but remain steadfast and spiritual. By analysing their stories, we uncover the impact of faith when dealing with entrepreneurship challenges.

Stories of successful Muslim entrepreneurs who have faced and overcome adversity

In Islamic history, during the era of the messenger of Allah, Prophet Muhammad (PBUH), he and several Muslim entrepreneurs faced and overcame significant adversity, setting examples of resilience and faith. Here are a few notable for inspiration:

Following Muhammad's (PBUH) journey, it is evident that adversity shaped him from a young age. While the other children received the love and care of their parents, Muhammad (PBUH) faced life's challenges alone. Despite this, his survival instinct thrived. Prophet Muhammad (PBUH) is a hero in Islamic history because he never gave up and confronted his issues head-on.

The Prophet's accomplishments as an entrepreneur can be attributed to his diligent labour and adept business management. A successful business requires several factors, including operating on trust, which is connected to ethics. The Quran's commandments served as the

Prophet's primary basis for conducting business and living his daily life. The Shariah governs the normative principles of business ethics that the Prophet taught and which are mentioned in the Quran.

All actions, whether good or evil, will ultimately have consequences. This is especially true in the business world, where a company's success or failure is heavily influenced by its ethical practices. Ethics are essential to anything in any sector since, although they may seem simple, people frequently break them, leading to the issue worsening on its own.

The Prophet (PBUH) experienced several challenging moments in his personal and communal life. Despite his great successes, his life was also incredibly difficult. With the help of Allah's will and guidance, he overcame all obstacles and emerged from the dark periods stronger than before.

Umm Salamah (RA) provides a powerful lesson about faith and resiliency. Despite her hardships—such as losing her husband and moving to Medina— she demonstrated incredible fortitude and a steadfast adherence to her religious beliefs. As one of the early believers, her unflinching fortitude in the face of hardship shows the value of perseverance and faith in Allah's guidance. Umm Salamah (RA) inspires us today to actively participate in constructive change, even when it means making a personal sacrifice, persevering through life's challenges, and holding fast to our faith in the face of adversity.

Moreover, Abu Bakr al-Siddiq, the first Caliph, remained steadfast in his faith despite losing wealth and business ties, using his resources to support the Muslim community. Uthman ibn Affan, the third Caliph, faced persecution but continued to prosper and generously provided a well for the Muslims in Medina. Abdur-Rahman ibn Awf rebuilt his fortune from scratch in Medina, contributing significantly to military campaigns and aiding the poor. Zubayr ibn al-Awwam, despite severe persecution, succeeded in trade and land investments, generously supporting the Muslim community. These stories highlight early Muslim entrepreneurs' resilience, faith, and contributions.

Impact of faith and spirituality on navigating entrepreneurial challenges

Relentless dedication and unceasing effort are two qualities commonly associated with entrepreneurship and are unquestionably necessary for reaching one's objectives. Despite monetary success, an overly preoccupied attitude toward hustle can lead to burnout, tension, and a feeling of hollowness. This is where spirituality and faith can provide balance.

When individuals are encouraged to cultivate inner harmony and serenity through spirituality, they are more likely to achieve a sense of balance between their personal lives and professional responsibilities. As a result, businesses prioritising promoting positive social impact are often spearheaded by entrepreneurs who integrate spiritual principles into their operational strategies.

Such leaders seek financial success and strive for meaningful and holistic growth for themselves and their communities. This mindset of incorporating spirituality in business practices can lead to more ethical decision-making, fostering a healthier and more sustainable work environment.

Finding one's greater mission and establishing a connection with a sense of meaning beyond the material world are common themes in spirituality. A distinct vision and a strong purpose are essential in entrepreneurship. Business ventures acquire a greater and more genuine meaning when they align with one's spiritual beliefs and ideals.

Simultaneously, faith frequently acts as a moral compass, guiding business owners through the maze of moral conundrums and obstacles that come with being in the business sector. It offers a fundamental structure within which virtues like honesty, compassion, and integrity are fostered and incorporated into business culture.

Spirituality and faith can both be sources of resiliency. These methods frequently focus on acceptance, flexibility, and the capacity to develop and learn from hardship. By incorporating these ideas and practices into their company journey, entrepreneurs can discover a deep sense of meaning, harmony, and persistence. This improves their personal well-being and creates more meaningful and long-lasting success.

Chapter Four

Islamic Business Ethics and Integrity

Islamic morality and ethics are fundamental to all facets of life, especially business. In this section, we will examine how these principles guide entrepreneurs in their endeavours, exploring the fundamentals of Islamic ethics in entrepreneurship.

Ethical Foundations of Islamic Business Practices

Islamic ethics mandate that its adherents fervently guard their actions, ideas, words, and intentions, as well as adhere to specific standards and codes of conduct in their social interactions, business dealings, family relationships, and interactions with neighbours, relatives, and friends. The Islamic ethical framework is distinct in affecting every aspect of human existence.

Islam emphasises the importance of rules and ethical business practices in daily life. Moral teachings on behaviour and acts, particularly in the economy, are commonly associated with Islam. These teachings can be categorised as positive or negative, right or wrong. Everything done will impact the realm of objective reality and the hereafter.

As mentioned earlier on in the book, Islam is more than just a "religion" in the narrow sense commonly used; it encompasses a holistic way of life. Therefore, ethics is something fundamental to it rather than just one aspect. The cornerstone of particular applications in economics is the larger Islamic ethics, which are rooted in the Islamic worldview. Let us examine these facets of economic activity further. The underlying precepts of Islamic business ethics are listed below.

Importance of honesty, trustworthiness, and fairness in Islamic entrepreneurship

Honesty

The term "honesty" is broad and has several connotations. It includes being truthful, performing one's obligations, being sincere at work, rendering impartial judgments and conclusions, keeping one's word, and more. Being truthful also entails acting appropriately and on schedule.

The Latin words honestus (honourable mention) and honos (honour), which denote honour, purity, and reputation, serve as the roots of the English term "honest". From this, we can infer that honesty is a suitable statement or behaviour that can be relied upon and positively impacts one's success. This integrity extends to one's voice as well as one's deeds. The quality that sets believers apart from hypocrites is honesty.

Islam strongly advocates honesty in business dealings and emphasises its essential role in maintaining social harmony and stability. In particular, Prophet Muhammad (SAW) stressed that the keys to success in business are honesty and treating consumers with kindness.

> *"The truthful and honest merchant is associated with the Prophets, the upright and the martyrs" (Al-Tirmidhi)*

> *In another hadith, Prophet Muhammad (PBUH) said: "God shows mercy to a person who is kindly when he sells, when he buys and when he makes a claim" (Al-Bukhari)*

The Quran emphasises the importance of truthfulness, integrity, and sincerity, particularly in Sharia law. Since deceit and dishonesty are frowned upon and prohibited, honesty is not merely required but declared vital. Both words and deeds demonstrate honesty. When someone acts, it undoubtedly reflects what is within them. Cheating is worse when it is done dishonestly. Those who lack honesty will resort to deception others whenever and wherever they see an opportunity. The Quran strongly prohibits lying.

Trustworthiness

Tawakkul, or "trust in God," is one of the most crucial mindsets in Islam. This is significant because faith requires confidence.

> *"If you are true believers, put your trust in God." (Quran 5:23)*

It is not surprising that Amana, the quality of being deserving of trust from both God and others, is one of the most prominent attitudes in social ethics. Amana and its roots indicate notions of trust rather than betrayal and safety rather than fear. In the Quran, Amana has three facets (1) as obligatory affairs (Quran, 8:27); as deposits (Quran, 4:58) and (3) as trustworthiness (honesty and integrity) (Quran, 28:26).

The Prophet of Allah was unique and exceptional in his reliability. He received praise for being "the Trustworthy One" (Amīn) even before he declared his prophetic status. Despite opposition to Islam at the time, even the Roman emperor inquired about the Prophet when he started urging people around the world to convert to Islam. He was praised for his moral integrity and unwavering dependability. Even amidst fierce adversaries in Makkah, individuals would still entrust their treasures to the last Prophet (PBUH).

> *The Holy Prophet (PBUH) stated that "a Muslim businessman who is truthful and trustworthy will be resurrected on the Day of Judgment alongside the martyrs" (Sunan Ibn Majah)*

Now, it can be seen that the cornerstones of Islamic business ethics are sincerity (*Sidq*) and dependability (*Amanah*). Numerous texts from the Quran and Hadith highlight these attributes, stressing the value of keeping one's word and being honest in all dealings. Muslim business owners are encouraged to be truthful in their interactions with partners, staff, or clients.

Fairness

Muslims are encouraged to conduct business with others in the way they want to be treated.

> *In the Quran, it is stated, "O you who have believed, be persistently standing firm in justice, witnesses for Allah, even if it be against yourselves or parents and relatives" (Quran, 4:135)*

> *The Holy Qur'an highlights the importance of justice in business: "And, O my people, give full measure and weight in justice, and do not deprive people of their due and do not commit abuse on the earth, spreading corruption" (Quran 11:85)*

In economic relations, Islamic ethics encourage justice (*Qist*) and fairness (*Adl*). This entails treating all parties involved fairly and ensuring no one falls victim to deceptive or unfair business practices. Treating suppliers and employees fairly, offering open contracts, and paying fair compensation are all crucial elements of conducting business in line with Islamic principles.

This is because Islamic teachings recommend and envisage that businesspeople justly price goods and services, share market share, and enter contracts in the marketplaces. Therefore, the spirit of fairness preserved in Islamic entrepreneurship assists in enhancing economic development and social welfare that aligns with justice in Islam.

It has been demonstrated that entrepreneurship plays a vital role in achieving the quality of self, society, and country. It is not merely a tool for improving living standards and societal conditions. Thus, the presence of entrepreneurs can contribute to shaping a contemporary, inventive, and creative society.

Islam is a religion that offers precepts for the betterment of human existence both here on Earth and in the Hereafter. The Quran expressly encourages individuals to work to survive in this world, particularly in business and entrepreneurship, which are thought to be the greatest occupations associated with the heritage of the Prophet Muhammad. Put another way, Islam urges every Muslim to start their business.

In terms of entrepreneurship, Muslim business owners seek to fulfil falah and offer social benefits to the larger community. Islam not only encourages Muslims to start their own businesses but also requires them to put in a lot of effort and overcome falah to meet their immediate needs to support society and Muslims as a whole. This is because business and entrepreneurship are highly compatible with the teachings of Islam.

Upholding integrity and ethical conduct in business transactions at an entrepreneur

In Islamic entrepreneurship, integrity is not compromised. Entrepreneurs are required to be truthful and maintain high ethical standards. This involves respecting contractual terms and conditions, meeting set responsibilities, and refraining from cheating or dishonesty. Maintaining integrity not only serves the entrepreneur's self-identity but also protects the stakeholders' self-interest.

Integrity, which is referred to in Arabic as "ihsan" or "sidq", is highly esteemed in the principles and doctrines of Islam. It speaks of honesty, authenticity, and upholding moral and ethical standards in all facets of one's life. Being honest in speaking is simply one aspect of integrity; another is acting with sincerity and consistent with one's principles and beliefs.

Upholding integrity can be challenging, and it is also clear that everyone wants to be treated with respect by others. What are some ways you, as a Muslim entrepreneur, can incorporate integrity into your everyday work routine? Here are some specific details to help you transition this concept into reality:

Be completely truthful: As a company, you must always speak the truth and disclose any information that can be helpful to clients and staff. And remember, acknowledge your mistakes!

Meet all your commitments: Customers demand things from you, whether explicitly promised or not. This demonstrates the value of your goods and services in effectively addressing their needs. Recognise these obligations and fulfil them at all costs.

Ultimately, Islam emphasises interior sincerity, honesty, and commitment to ethical ideals as key components of integrity, transcending outward appearances. As a Muslim entrepreneur, these values should form your character and conduct across every aspect of life.

The primary principles of commerce

The core ideas of commerce are articulated as follows in Islamic teachings:

- Ensure precise weight and measure in transactions.
- Avoid bringing evil into the world to cause trouble.
- Respect others' rights and give individuals what is rightfully theirs.
- Find contentment with God-given remaining money after fulfilling obligations to others rather than coveting excess wealth.

With security and peace, commerce can thrive, emphasising the importance of fairness and honesty in business interactions. It's essential to lavishly grant others their due and engage in transactions that are entirely honest and deemed favourable by God. Avoiding accusations of selfish greed or profiteering is crucial, as well as fostering unhindered and unrestricted trade among different regions while maintaining the tranquillity of the land.

It is important to remember that justice is a superior virtue. Giving others fair weight and measure equates to treating them fairly and justly, much as the Messenger of Allah (PBUH) conducted business exclusively in accordance with the principles of justice and truth. He consistently encouraged genuine empathy and consideration between the buyer and the seller. All deals involving any unfairness or hardship for the seller or the buyer have his vehement disapproval.

Islam expects its adherents to conduct business with a noble attitude of justice blended with human kindness, denouncing all forms of unfairness and abuse in human connections. "Ta'auanu ala birri wa't-taqwa" (mutual cooperation for the cause of righteousness or piety) should be the foundation of all dealings. *Insaf* (justice) and (magnanimity) should be present in a seller's behaviour during a transaction.

> *Holy Prophet (PBUH) said: "God will forgive the sins of a Muslim who absolves a fellow Muslim from a sale contract not liked by the latter." (Ibn Majah)*

Lust for wealth and an ignoble ambition to rise in status are the driving forces behind illegal trade. Islam offers an alternative standard for judging a person's status that targets the source of the desire for wealth.

Let us now discuss the types of business dealings forbidden in Islamic law. In addition to criticising certain commercial practices, the Holy Prophet (PBUH) established several prerequisites that must be met for every transaction to be considered legitimate. Some of these forbidden practices include:

Lawful acquisition of goods and payment: Both the items to be sold and the amount to be paid for them should be legitimately obtained and expressly stated. The products being sold must be acquired legally. Selling items one has taken or obtained dishonestly is not a legitimate business practice. Additionally, nothing should be bought with cash obtained through dishonest means or taken as illicit pleasure. Under this condition, both the seller and the buyer are accountable for ensuring the legality of the goods and money involved in the transaction.

Sale of items in the open market: Products for sale should be offered in an open marketplace, and sellers must be informed about the market status before offers are made by buyers to buy. Sellers need to know market circumstances and prices to prevent buyers from taking advantage of their ignorance.

Possession before sale: Muslims are advised by the Holy Prophet (PBUH) not to engage in advance transactions, which entails selling commodities before gaining control of them.

> *The Holy Prophet (may peace be upon him) states, "Whoever buys cereals shall not sell them until he has obtained their possession" (Sahih al-Bukhari)*

Ibn 'Abbas asserts that the same principles that apply to cereals also apply to other types of goods.

> *The Holy Prophet (peace be upon him) has said, "Bargain not about that which is not with you."*

Only commodities and things deemed halal (lawful) may be traded by Muslims. Trade and trafficking in items that Islam prohibits are not permitted. For instance, trading in wine, pigs, animal corpses, and idols is prohibited. Additionally, since it is against the law for women to utilise thin, transparent clothing, a pious Muslim businessperson should not deal with such items.

Furthermore, certain restrictions apply to the trade of specific animal parts. For instance, while the sale of an animal's carcass is prohibited, certain parts, like the skin, may be sold for lawful purposes, such as making shoes. Although, the flesh of deceased animals cannot be sold. In Islam, the tusks of an elephant are no different from the valuable skin of other animals.

In summary, Islam encourages all Muslim businesspersons to treat all parties fairly in transactions. Anything beneficial to one but detrimental to the other is unacceptable. The buyer is prohibited from unfairly taking advantage of the seller's ignorance; likewise, the seller is expected to disclose any item faults to the buyer.

Aligning Business Goals with Moral Values

Establishing ethical and sustainable business processes requires balancing corporate objectives with moral principles. Every Muslim should have moral principles and values that direct their behaviour, conduct, and actions so they do not stray from the guidelines that Allah (SWT) has established.

Every Muslim uses these moral precepts and values as a foundation and a source of guidance when engaging in economic activities like management, commerce, consumption, production, and distribution. A trader can be successful if they work hard at their business and uphold strong moral and ethical ideals.

Furthermore, these moral principles can direct all human conduct and action in all economic endeavours, such as accumulating wealth, pursuing financial gain, handling business dealings in accordance with Shariah, etc. Every religion and teaching in the world always exhorts its adherents to uphold and put into practice moral principles.

Every religion's moral principles direct its adherents towards moral behaviour, including business dealings. Islam is one among them; it places a strong emphasis on moral principles, Islamic ethics (*akhlaq*), and the virtues of moral life in all of its adherents.

Every merchant needs to be guided in their commercial dealings by principles and values that apply to all Muslims. A Muslim trader with strong morals and values is one who succeeds in the market. This section will discuss a business's morals and values.

Integrating Islamic principles of justice and accountability into business operations

The idea of justice in all facets of human existence is one of Islam's gifts to humanity. Islam teaches that justice can be applied to all aspects of life, including business.

The administration of law in accordance with established and recognised standards is referred to as "justice." It is also understood as allocating everyone their proper share and placing everything in its proper position at the proper time, level, and manner—without any excess, unhappiness, or delay. Among the values that the Quran and the statements of the Prophet emphasise are the concepts of kindness and fairness. Islamic economics strongly emphasises the concept of justice, or "adl." This virtue is necessary in social, moral, legal, and commercial dealings.

Like truth, justice is a divine virtue. Islam is as persistent in upholding this ideal as the truth. The Quran places a strong emphasis on the virtue of justice. Yet, the Prophet has frequently urged Muslims to uphold the ideal of ihsan, characterised by kindness, generosity, and expertise.

While the absence of adl harms people and jeopardises peace and harmony, the absence of ihsan harms no one. It implies a less severe stance than what justice demands; it begins where the boundaries of justice end.

At the same time, Islam also establishes rules on accountability, particularly in the state's administration and at the community level. Leaders, such as caliphs, are accountable for their actions vertically to those they govern and horizontally to their peers.

Similarly, individuals in management are also subject to both vertical and horizontal accountability. Islam emphasises accountability as a crucial facet of management.

Entrepreneurs who undertake financial risks in their ventures must manage every aspect of their business to ensure its success. According to Islamic teachings, every individual will be held accountable for their actions, whether they are good or harmful, and will get the appropriate rewards or punishments.

In the context of business, the governing board of directors is the entity to which management is answerable for their obligations. The beneficiaries and stakeholders play a role in holding the board accountable, ensuring transparency and ethical conduct within the organisation.

> *"Whosoever does good equal to the weight of an atom (or a small ant) shall see it. And whosoever does evil equal to the weight of an atom (or a small ant) shall see it."*
> *(Quran, 99:7-8)*

The principles of Islamic law, as transmitted by the Holy Prophet (SAW), are timeless and applicable to all people, with rulings drawn from the Quran, the Hadith, and other legal sources. All Muslim business endeavours should be based on these principles first to establish a relationship with Allah SWT and then pursue worldly gain through constitutional and lawful means as directed by Allah SWT. The ultimate goal is to seek Allah's favour and respect in the Afterlife.

When Islamic principles are applied to business operations, the primary focus changes from merely maximising profit to seeking Allah SWT's pleasure. Clear guidelines on what is right and wrong help businesses outperform competitors and grow at a.

Demonstrating ethical leadership and responsibility in entrepreneurship

Being an ethical leader is more than just following the law. It is about establishing a precedent from the top by upholding moral conduct in all facets of company operations. This encompasses the values that were previously covered in-depth:

Integrity: Even under difficult circumstances, ethical leaders should behave honourably and openly.

Accountability: They demand moral behaviour from both themselves and other people.

Fairness: Ethical leaders ensure decisions are made impartially and treat employees with respect.

Social responsibility: They consider the broader impact of their decisions on the community, employees, and environment in addition to financial gain.

There are many reasons to lead with ethics. Ethical leaders have the ability and power to inspire those around them to act with integrity. By offering clear guidelines, they positively influence many individuals and contribute to the common good. When one leads by example and guides moral behaviour, others will take note and follow suit.

Ethical entrepreneurs understand they are the custodians of resources and agents of change. Thus, they focus on the welfare of society and the environment. Ethical leadership and responsibility in the case of an entrepreneur foster credibility among the stakeholders and help in building sustainable businesses. Integrating business objectives with moral standards is critical in Islamic business venturing, as integrity, responsibility, and ethical management are some hallmarks of business practices.

Through the application of Islamic principles in business, managers design an ethical structure through which they execute their operations. By adhering to justice, integrity, and social responsibility, ethical entrepreneurs play a role in enhancing justice, fairness, and a sustainable society, hence enriching Islamic values in today's society.

Chapter Five

Entrepreneurial Mindset and Innovation

The current corporate environment is characterised by intense energy and quick evolution. Because of this, companies have to compete fiercely to survive in an increasingly competitive market. Undoubtedly, innovative methods are now essential to any organisation's long-term development and success. How can businesses implement innovation to keep ahead of the competition? Here, having an entrepreneurial mindset is crucial.

An entrepreneurial mentality is a collection of abilities, perspectives, and methods that help you spot opportunities, overcome obstacles, and accomplish goals in a range of contexts. Simply put, "bringing ideas to life in the market" is the basic interpretation of an entrepreneurial mindset.

The creative, visionary, and action-oriented mindset that underpins entrepreneurship is what turns ideas into tangible results. The entrepreneurial attitude emphasises unrelenting personal development, accepting responsibility for failures, and utilising lessons learned and willpower to reach new heights. Whether you are just starting on your path, leading a large organisation, or taking a risk, you can use your entrepreneurial attitude as a force to create transformation at every level.

Based on the analysis of hadith and the Qur'an, several traits define the mindset of an Islamic entrepreneur:

Ethical

Islam holds that a business should operate with the principles of mutual benefit—both material and moral—consensual and trust in its purchasing and selling. Imam Ghazali asserts that a Muslim engaging in trading as a career or launching his own company must first follow the laws governing business dealings as outlined in the Islamic Shariah.

This can be accomplished by implementing an understandable and workable transactional agreement, which consists of the buyer's wanted products (clearly qualified and quantified) and the seller's desired currency, or money, which is determined by the nominal value that has been agreed upon.

The Holy Quran has emphasised how crucial ethics is in business:

> "And, O my people, gives full measure and weight justly and defrauds not men of their things, and act not corruptly in the land making mischief. What remains with Allah is better for you, if you are believers" (Quran, 85-86)

Optimistic

An enterprising person with optimism embraces calculated risks, aiming to achieve a clear long-term vision for the business's future. This mindset allows entrepreneurs to remain highly motivated and dedicated, even in the face of unfulfilled expectations. Without a doubt, the upbeat idea always resides in God: "Bismillahi tawakkaltu alallahi"

Honest

Refusing to engage in Gharar (unclear or deceptive business practices) means daring to disclose the true nature of their ventures and striving to conduct their operations to the best of their abilities. This approach is crucial, as it instils great confidence in purchasers and business partners, increasing their likelihood of becoming long-term consumers.

Caring

True entrepreneurs prioritise not only the rapid growth of their company but also the creation of a strong network based on mutual collaboration to achieve wealth for everyone involved. Successful entrepreneurs view their business success as a testament to their worship and a valuable asset in the hereafter.

Thus, an Islamic entrepreneur should embrace the idea of compassion, understanding that wealth accumulated in this world should be shared with the underprivileged. By doing so, they can reap the benefits of their generosity in the hereafter.

Independent

Islamic entrepreneurs view their work as something that is "to be done" (biyadihi).

> *In the Quran, it is stated, "And say, 'Do [as you will], for Allah will see your deeds, and [so will] His Messenger and the believers. And you will be returned to the Knower of the unseen and the witnessed, and He will inform you of what you used to do.'" (Quran 9:105)*

This encourages them to actively seek God's gifts (rizki) upon receiving His blessings.

> *The Holy Prophet Muhammad (peace be upon him) said, "Indeed, seeking lawful sustenance is a duty after the obligatory prayers" (Tabrani and Bayhaqi)*

It is clear from the above that people should work hard and lead independent lives.

Flexible

Being flexible means being easily adjustable, non-rigid, and awkward. Put another way, adaptable business owners are always adept at changing with the times and the environment, demonstrating imagination and creativity, recognising themselves as individuals but also as beings of God, appreciating their status and adhering to regular prayer. Prayer, a way to relinquish control to God, allows them to ask for their desires and accept whatever outcomes God provides.

These wise words have a profound meaning: adaptable business owners can balance their life between the world and the hereafter, work hard to boost company success and productivity and amass as much wealth as possible because they won't die.

However, they will promptly leave work at the sound of the call to prayer to perform both the required and sunnah prayers. This reflects the belief that "God makes the decisions, but man strives toward them." Praying is, therefore, one of the treatments for striving for this ideal.

When prosperity abounds, and the fruits of labour are plentiful, fulfilling zakat obligations, aiding the underprivileged, and donating generously from the abundance of one's labour is vital. This mindset prepares for the Afterlife, living as though death could come any day. As a result, an adaptable entrepreneur can adjust to both the here and the afterlife.

Cultivating an Innovative Mindset in Islamic Entrepreneurship

Islamic entrepreneurship fosters the development of an innovation culture based on the principles of Islam. Originality and innovation are not only encouraged but appreciated as examples of artistic genius and divine intervention. Entrepreneurs are urged to unlock their innovation to meet social demands, redefine issues, and co-create value for themselves and society. Let us first look at the value of creativity and innovation in Islam.

In pre-Islamic Arabia, ignorance was widespread before the arrival of Islam. The Quran instructed Muslims to be innovative and to apply their inventiveness in line with Islamic values and Sharia law, as well as for the well of humanity.

The acts of innovating and producing something new are the two meanings associated with the word bidah. The well-known hadith are used to support the argument against creativity when bidah is used to stifle innovation and creativity:

> *"If somebody innovates something which is not in harmony with the principles of our religion, that thing is rejected" (Sahih Bukhari)*

As a result, the Prophet (PBUH) accepted bidah and only objected to it when it did not conform to Islam. This Hadith further affirms that innovations and ideas are acceptable as long as they follow Islamic law.

Creativity and innovation are essential for business success. They allow business owners to stand out from the competition, adapt to shifting market conditions, solve issues, spur growth, take calculated risks, attract stakeholders, and promote a continuous improvement culture.

If entrepreneurs conducted business in the same manner across all markets, industries, and product and service categories, no one would have an edge over others, and many enterprises would fail quickly. All things considered, originality and creativity are essential to entrepreneurship success. They enable business owners to identify opportunities, resolve issues, set themselves apart, respond to shifts, make consistent improvements, and propel the expansion of their enterprises.

In a business environment that is constantly changing, entrepreneurs can create profitable companies by embracing innovation and cultivating an inventive attitude.

Embracing creativity and problem-solving inspired by Islamic teachings

Muslims are encouraged to be creative and to apply their imagination in line with Islamic ideals and Sharia law, as well as for the betterment of humanity, by the Quran. The Quran established a framework that enabled Muslims to concentrate on improving people's lives and society by developing novel theories and concepts.

The Quran encouraged creativity by giving Muslims deeper understanding and inspiration through creative examples. Prophet Muhammad (PBUH) realised that Muslims might consult Islamic scholars knowledgeable about the Quran, hadith, and Sunnah if they had any questions or needed clarification. The Quran contains all the answers. The Prophet (PBUH) expected Muslims to be literate and to continue learning throughout their lives. Islam has always supported individualism, ingenuity, creativity, technology, and any invention that advances well-being.

> *Allah says: "O you who have believed, bow and prostrate and worship your Lord and do well that you may succeed," (Quran 22:77)*

Creativity fuels innovation and problem-solving, which also shapes the future of our planet. Accepting creativity allows individuals to think outside the box, overcome obstacles, and generate ideas that have the potential to change people's lives and entire societies.

As a Muslim entrepreneur, establishing a creative culture inside your company is essential to fostering innovation. Leaders should promote an environment that welcomes innovation and pushes for trial and error, even in the face of potential failure. You can maximise team productivity and spur innovation by fostering a secure environment where workers may freely express their ideas. This entails fostering an atmosphere where your employees are encouraged to take chances and share their thoughts.

Fostering transparent dialogue and appreciating varied viewpoints can stimulate original thought and inventiveness. Although creative thinking can solve problems, combined with interest, work, and teamwork, it can develop original and useful solutions for any problem.

Encouraging entrepreneurship as a means of social and economic innovation

In Islamic teachings, entrepreneurship is considered an effective social and economic change instrument.

Economic development and entrepreneurship work hand in hand, with creativity serving as a growth-promoting agent. Innovation, entrepreneurship, and economic development have a symbiotic relationship since they both foster and assist one another in the following ways:

- In entrepreneurship, innovation frequently results in the creation of more effective procedures, tools, and techniques. These procedures, tools, and techniques boost productivity and result in better output and faster economic growth.

- Creative business owners frequently launch new ventures or grow already existing ones, which inevitably results in the creation of new jobs.

- Offering innovative products and services can give companies a competitive advantage in the market. Profitability, market share, and sales may all rise as a result.

- Economies that encourage entrepreneurship and innovation are better equipped to compete globally. They are more equipped to handle economic obstacles because they can adjust to shifting market dynamics, developments, and technology with greater ease.

In sum, the relationship between innovation, entrepreneurship, and economic development is a virtuous cycle. This symbiotic relationship ensures economies remain vibrant, resilient, and capable of sustained growth.

Simultaneously, entrepreneurship serves as a primary catalyst for the advancement and progress of society. Economic growth and the creation of jobs are two of entrepreneurship's most important social effects. Successful and expanding businesses create jobs and boost the economy. Therefore, entrepreneurship has the potential to be extremely important in promoting economic growth and raising societal standards of life.

Innovation and the development of technology are two other important effects of entrepreneurship on society. Entrepreneurs are renowned for their innovative and forward-thinking methods. They frequently introduce novel concepts and goods to the market that have the power to upend established markets and alter our way of life. For instance, the Internet and the growth of the tech sector have revolutionised communication and information access while creating many new jobs.

The future is shaped by entrepreneurship, which also propels technological and innovative developments that can significantly impact society. To sum up, entrepreneurship has the ability to significantly contribute to the resolution of a number of the most pressing social issues, including resolving social and environmental concerns, fostering economic growth and creating jobs. By harnessing the inventive nature and problem-solving abilities of entrepreneurs, we have the potential to build a more promising and sustainable future for everybody.

We have seen that Islam enables individuals to own businesses as a means to stimulate economic growth, fight poverty, and promote social equity. Entrepreneurs are encouraged to innovate not only for profit but also to positively impact society by applying their knowledge and developments to address societal challenges.

Furthermore, Islamic entrepreneurship stresses the aspects of ethical behaviour and social responsibility in generating innovation. The creation of new values is encouraged to be done in a sustainable and ethical manner, and the external environment of society and the natural world is to be considered. This way, applying the main principles of justice, compassion, and stewardship to their business initiatives, they positively influence the development of society.

Although there are many moving parts in the relationship between initiative and economic development, most people agree that entrepreneurship is essential to economic development and growth. Entrepreneurship produces a more inventive and efficient economy, which also fosters competition and the creation of new companies and jobs. Numerous initiatives have been launched to apply the tenets of entrepreneurship to create a more equitable and sustainable world, particularly as a result of certain entrepreneurs' growing social consciousness.

It is therefore crucial for Islamic entrepreneurship to develop an innovation culture in order to promote social and economic development. Through creativity, problem-solving and Islamic values of ethical entrepreneurship, business leaders can harness innovations to drive economic change with solutions to existing problems.

Leveraging Technology for Halal Innovation

The application of technology and the incorporation of Islamic values in the business world have led to the discovery of new opportunities for improved growth. Global civilisation changed from being industrial to informational with the introduction of personal computers and the Internet, where ICTs became ubiquitous, and information processing became the main focus.

The twenty-first century's technological advances in communication and information have stoked innumerable futuristic visions of a world ruled by people and justice. ICTs have affected every aspect of human life in the modern era. Thanks to these technologies, people from every walk of life can now connect and communicate in a highly connected world, transcending time and location.

The combination of Islamic values with technological approaches provides a good chance to meet the needs of Muslims and act ethically. Technology can, therefore, be used by entrepreneurs to create new products as well as services that conform to the halal standard of doing business.

Let us look at the possibilities of using technology to drive halal innovation, emphasising the combination of Islamic values with technological concepts in business.

Integrating Islamic values with technology-driven solutions in business

Solutions based on technology play a critical role in improving the whole halal ecosystem. Technology can be used to improve the halal industry by increasing efficiency, authenticity, and transparency. The information technology industry's rapid advancement produces new services in the form of technological applications.

For instance, the rise in technology supporting and enhancing Sharia compliance for businesses directly results from expanding Sharia-compliant financing services. Sharia-compliant fintech has become a catalyst for innovation, guaranteeing that companies may function effectively while adhering to Islamic financing regulations.

Businesses can also employ technology to encourage their customers and clients to engage in more ethical and socially conscious financial practices. By utilising technology, Sharia-compliant companies can maintain compliance while staying ahead of the fintech boom.

Combining Islamic values with technological approaches provides a good chance to meet Muslims' needs and act ethically. Entrepreneurs can, therefore, use technology to create new products and services that conform to the halal standard of doing business.

Fintech, or Sharia-compliant financial technology, is the term used to describe technological solutions that respect Islamic finance regulations on Sharia-compliant services and transactions. Fintech can be defined as cutting-edge technology or online tools such as blockchain, internet banking, Sharia compliance banking, artificial intelligence, and apps that help Muslim-owned enterprises.

One of the most important aspects of Sharia-compliant finance is the connection between ethics and technology. Since social justice and ethics are the cornerstones of Islamic finance, technologies must also play a part in enforcing and amplifying ethical standards. Technological solutions make compliance automation, improved risk assessment and mitigation, real-time tracking, increased monitoring, and reporting possible. All of them are in line with Sharia law and the moral principles of Islamic finance.

Another example of this integration is the incorporation of mobile applications that facilitate the delivery of halal foods, allowing consumers to access halal-certified products easily. These apps not only simplify the process of verifying the halal status of food products in the market but also help consumers make informed decisions based on their faith.

In addition, technology can also be applied to make the supply chain more transparent, ensuring that products produced, processed, and distributed are halal as required. For example, blockchain technology can trace the origin of halal products, providing customers with confidence in their authenticity and halal status.

Technological developments have opened up many new avenues for corporate expansion. Of these recent advancements, machine learning has drawn interest from companies all around the world. All businesses, regardless of size—from startups to well-known labels—aspire to keep up with the most recent developments in the marketing industry.

AI will increase productivity by saving business owners time and money. This is the ideal opportunity for them to update their halal enterprise and stay on top of this trend. AI can be used to ensure product safety, streamline the halal clearance process, and cater to the needs of halal consumers.

Blockchain technology can improve and streamline this procedure for increased efficiency. A distributed ledger called blockchain makes safe and open record-keeping possible. Blockchain technology ensures the integrity of the supply chain by allowing halal certification authorities to create an unchangeable record of the entire process, from the source of raw ingredients to the final product. By putting these safeguards in place, fraud risk can be reduced, and the legitimacy of halal products can be ensured.

Technology may greatly impact e-commerce, which is a developing field. halal enterprises can now reach a global audience thanks to e-commerce. E-commerce has many advantages but drawbacks, such as the possibility of fraud and the difficulty of confirming whether an item is halal when purchased online. To overcome the aforementioned challenges, halal e-commerce platforms can utilise cutting-edge technology, such as blockchain and AI, to confirm the legitimacy and compliance of their product offerings.

Technology helps companies organise their approach and ensures they stay true to the tenets of Islamic financing. It provides real-time data, which increases efficiency and accuracy. Sharia compliance is frequently automatable in the IT platforms used by the healthcare industry.

Exploring opportunities for innovation in halal industries and markets

The prospect of the halal industry is vast, with opportunities for innovation in sectors such as food and beverage, pharmaceuticals, cosmetics, and finance. Entrepreneurs should capitalise on these opportunities by thinking out of the box and developing products and services tailored to the needs of Muslims.

For example, there is a growing consumer preference for halal products in the food industry, including plant-based meats and dairy-free products. Through technology and innovation, halal-certified products can be developed to meet the demands of Muslim consumers while also appealing to other audiences.

In finance, Islamic fintech startups use technology to deliver Shariah-compliant solutions like Islamic finance, P2P lending, and crowdfunding. These innovations help Muslims facilitate financial services according to their religion and promote financial inclusion and ethical banking.

Using technology in halal innovation offers new prospects for businesses to serve Muslim customers while being halal compliant. Incorporating technology into halal business practices means that entrepreneurs can create programs that ensure that their business practices are halal, ensuring transparency, integrity, and ethicality in their businesses. Since the halal industry is continuously expanding and developing, technology will be a crucial factor for competitiveness and international development in markets.

1. Strategic Planning and Goal Setting

Strategic management comprises defining the organisation's goals, devising plans and policies to accomplish them, allocating resources to execute the strategies, and offering overall guidance for the business. The company's top management formulates and implements long-term goals and initiatives through strategic management. These decisions are made after considering resources and evaluating the internal and external contexts in which the business competes.

Muslim entrepreneurs can draw lessons and knowledge from their history when designing a tactical strategy for the future. Throughout the Prophet Muhammad's (PUBH) history, numerous episodes highlight the innate talent and personal skills Almighty Allah bestowed upon him. From these episodes and how he handled them, there are countless lessons and valuable wisdom to be cherished.

All organisations use strategic planning to help them focus their resources, establish priorities, and improve their overall operations. Strategic planning is essential to ensure that stakeholders and employees are working towards shared objectives. There will be consensus on the planned outcomes and results as well as these shared aims. In reaction to a changing environment, it also assists the organisation in evaluating and modifying its course.

The Quran constantly reminds us that Allah SWT is the greatest planner. For example, in the Quran, Allah discusses His preparation and the indications of His Perfect Plan.

> *"Do you not see that Allah sends down rain from the sky, and we produce thereby fruits of varying colours? And in the mountains are tracts, white and red of varying shades and [some] extremely black. And among people*

and moving creatures and grazing livestock are various colours similarly. Only those fear Allah, from among His servants, who have knowledge. Indeed, Allah is Exalted in Might and Forgiving." (Quran, 28-29)

Strategic Decision-Making Based on Islamic Principles

Every individual must regularly make decisions for both their professional and private needs. This process is crucial but labour-intensive and is a fundamental aspect of life on Earth. Every Muslim has the responsibility to consider Islamic teachings when making decisions to avoid negatively impacting humanity or society at large. Decision-making involves selecting a plan of action from two or more viable options to address a particular problem.

When discussing decision-making, it is common to concentrate on the decision or the decision-making process itself. While we are focused on the decision itself, it is helpful to observe the range of interpretations available for the term "decision." For instance, according to one definition, "to make a decision is to deliberate over several options before deciding what one should do in a particular situation." Although challenging, the procedure is efficient.

Divine law sets the limits on the use of power, and consultation is required. Strategic decision-making based on Islamic principles integrates ethical, moral, and spiritual considerations into the decision-making process, aligning business practices with the teachings of Islam. Here's an overview of how these principles can be applied in business planning:

Utilising Tawakkul (reliance on God) and Istikharah (prayer for guidance) when business planning

So far in this book, we have established that dependence on Allah will determine success and enjoyment more than any techniques, abilities, or business methods. Now, it is time to embrace what Muslims refer to as Tawakkul.

Within Islamic thinking, Tawakkul—an Arabic term that loosely translates to "reliance" or "trust in God"—is a profound idea. It represents a well-rounded way of living in which self-reliance and faith in a higher force coexist in harmony. This idea may be applied outside of religious settings and is a powerful mental model for negotiating life's uncertainties.

Understanding the Tawakkul model helps enhance decision-making, promote resilience, and lessen anxiety. As a Muslim entrepreneur, you can incorporate Tawakkul into your psychological model toolset in the following ways:

Let us contemplate the uncertain domain of business planning and imagine making financial investment decisions. Here, you carry out your due diligence by studying the industry, examining trends, and varying your holdings. The movement of the market is still unpredictable, though. In this sense, Tawakkul refers to making wise choices while acknowledging the possibility of loss and seeing it as a necessary step in the investing process rather than a disastrous occurrence.

You may have to put in a lot of work when it comes to career planning, including learning necessary skills, networking, applying, and getting ready for interviews. However, whether you get the job or not is ultimately determined by factors outside of your control. Tawakkul practice here would entail giving it your all and persevering no matter what happens, realising that losing the job could just be a diversion to something greater rather than a failure.

Tawakkul is key to happiness and is essential for maintaining an optimistic outlook on life and business. Take a step back from your work, reflect on Allah, and remind yourself:

"Ya Allah, I appreciate this path you have carved out for me. I am aware that my path is unique from everyone else's. I know it might have taken this individual a year to accumulate a million dollars, but my goodness, I do not care if it takes me five or ten. Whatever path you have planned for me, I believe in it. I am confident that it will materialise. I will gladly follow whatever route you have planned for me and overcome any challenges you may have put in my way to teach me lessons. I will also take pleasure in the entire experience."

We need to be upbeat and full of faith in Allah.

In addition, Istikharah is a form of prayer in Islam in which one turns to Allah when faced with a choice or important decision. Muslims can apply Istikharah in business decision-making, as it helps individuals seek guidance from Allah in their endeavours.

The Arabic meaning of the word Istikhara is "seeking guidance from Allah." Istikhara is so significant that the Prophet Muhammad (PBUH) instructed Muslims to recite it for every significant issue. As an entrepreneur, you may encounter numerous unforeseen circumstances that require careful planning and difficult choices. However, if you wish to seek wisdom from Allah, you must request his help from the Dua e Istikhara. This method involves asking Allah to guide you in making the best decision and determining if a certain undertaking will benefit you both here on Earth and in the Hereafter. To perform Istikhara, there are particular procedures Muslims must follow to ask Allah for assistance.

First, you must ensure you have true and pure intentions. Seeking guidance from Allah and making decisions that are best for your material and spiritual welfare should be your main priorities.

After two mandatory prayer rakahs, you should perform the Dua e Istikhara. For Allah's guidance and blessings, you must also pray and recite the dua (Istikhara supplication) following the optional prayer. The dua says:

O Allah, I pray for Your guidance based on Your wisdom, Your support based on Your might, and Your boundless favour because, as I say, You are capable while I am not, You are aware of things I am not, and You are the Knower of the Hidden. O Allah, grant me guidance, support, and blessings in this particular commercial endeavour if You are aware that it will benefit me in terms of my faith, means of subsistence, and ultimate goal. And please turn this subject away from me as well as me away from it if you know that it will hurt my faith, my livelihood, ultimately my end. And whatever the good may be, decree it for me, and satisfy me with it.

Istikhara's guidance might be revealed in several ways. It can be an unexplainable incident, dream, or intuition. It is imperative to pay attention to these indications since they will help you reflect Allah's direction. By engaging in Istikhara, you show your dependence on Allah and accept that only He can guide you in the best direction.

When making business decisions, it is critical to exercise patience, have faith in Allah's wisdom, and keep in mind that ultimately success comes from Allah's blessings.

Setting achievable and impactful goals aligned with Islamic values

From the moment we register in undergraduate business school until we finish a Master's degree, we are taught SMART goals. A SMART goal is time-bound, realistic, measurable, and specific.

Islam encourages Muslims to adopt goals that benefit not only the community and society at large but also themselves. Muslims should make an effort to connect their objectives with the welfare of humanity as a whole. Setting objectives, however, must be done in accordance with the Quran and Sunnah, keeping in mind that Allah is the ultimate planner and that we are not allowed to make grandiose statements.

The message of the Prophet Muhammad (PBUH) was endowed by Allah with a purposeful objective. The Prophet's ultimate goal was to disseminate the Word of Islam, which is Allah's message of monotheism, or the belief in a single God. The Prophet's long- and short-term objectives were perfect because Allah revealed them through Divine Wisdom. Thus, when we examine the Sunnah, we are aware that what we are witnessing is Allah's decision-making process, as it is reflected in the life of a model citizen.

The Prophet Muhammad practised moderation in everything he did. According to his Hadith and Sunnah, he was precise in delivering the word of Allah to an uninformed audience. The growing number of believers who returned to Islam made his ambitions measurable. His vision and mission were action-oriented, whether preaching, organising a fight, helping the underprivileged, or spending time with friends and family. Because of his realism, millions of people accepted Islam.

They could identify with him and his beliefs. His speech was not pretentious or insincere, in contrast to other beliefs prevalent in the society at the time. In summary, he always understood the value of timing, which contributed to Islam's triumph and the expansion of Allah's Name and Message via discourse, conflict, communities, and, eventually, the entire world. Make sure your company's goals are SMART as well.

By setting goals and tracking their progress, businesses can benefit in the following ways:

- A precise, succinct, and widely accepted definition of success, especially when goals are created to help achieve corporate objectives.

- A framework for more accurately gauging responsibility since it allows business divisions, teams, and employees to be evaluated based on how well they achieved the set goals.

- The ideal method for inspiring and involving every worker.
- An approach to convey priorities and synchronise employees, groups, and business divisions that might not otherwise understand how their tasks fit into accomplishing the company's objectives.

Furthermore, when it comes to strategic management, goal setting must be practical and specific to the business. Goals should be realistic and within the range of what an entrepreneur, considering their strengths, resources, and market conditions, can achieve in a given period.

Moreover, in the realm of strategic management, it is crucial that goal setting is not only practical but also highly specific to the business at hand. This means that goals should not be vague or overly ambitious but rather grounded in reality and attainable within a defined timeframe.

By considering these factors, individuals can develop a strategic plan that sets achievable goals and increases the likelihood of long-term success for their business venture. By developing goals and measures for what constitutes achievement, Muslim business owners can keep track of performance, change strategy and techniques, and maintain a sense of purpose.

Time Management and Productivity in Islamic Entrepreneurship

Managing one's time well is a valuable skill that has been highly valued in Islam. Effective time management is emphasised in both the Quran and the Hadith, and it is essential to being a successful and productive Muslim. Effective time management might be difficult, but it is necessary for living a more fruitful and satisfying life. Islam views time as a precious gift from Allah Almighty, and it is up to us to manage it well.

The Islamic notion of Barakah, or the favours from Allah, is one of the most important parts of time management. This implies that Allah would reward a Muslim who manages their time well with even more time to succeed and fulfil their objectives. On the other hand, a Muslim who wastes time forfeits Barakah and has less productive and efficient use of their time.

Time is an invaluable resource and a highly significant Amana from Allah (SWT). Time well spent brings prosperity in this world and everlasting happiness in the next. Since we only have so much time, we must make the most of it to achieve lasting success. Islam has also contributed significantly to time management education through the teachings of the Holy Quran and the sayings of the Prophet Muhammad (PBUH). Businesses must manage their time well since it affects their production. Without effective time management, many fail. Therefore, it is vital for us to manage time properly.

Time management is important not only in our professional lives but in our private ones, too. The act of scheduling and exerting reasonable control over the amount of time spent on particular tasks, particularly to boost effectiveness, efficiency, or productivity, is referred to as time management.

Over time, it has gained enormous importance, and many people have realised that it is a significant problem that affects many facets of life. Effective time management is crucial for organisations since it directly affects productivity; many fail to manage their time well.

The art of time management involves planning, organising, budgeting, and scheduling one's time to produce more productive and efficient work. It is an integrated concept that considers all people, places, and times. Its use is not restricted to particular administrators or locations.

Additionally, the idea of time has been closely linked to administrative tasks in business. These tasks require constant planning, analysis, and assessment of every activity people engage in during their regular working hours to maximise the time allocated to achieving objectives.

Everyone needs to comprehend the value and purpose of time and learn how to use it wisely for their advancement, development, and growth—avoiding the bad effects of wasting or spending it in vain. Muslims are supposed to take time seriously, and they are responsible for ensuring that time is used appropriately.

Balancing work-life commitments through effective time management

The delicate tango between work-related obligations and personal pursuits is known as work-life balance. It entails time management to maintain productivity and success without letting work consume the rest of your day. Everybody has a varied understanding of this idea; it varies based on their requirements, interests, obligations to their families, and the demands of their careers. Recall that the objective is to strike a balance so that you can be fulfilled and content in both your personal and professional life without becoming overburdened.

Maintaining an appropriate balance between work and life is mostly dependent on knowing how to manage your time well. By carefully planning and allocating your hours between work and personal activities, you can design a balanced schedule where work and personal activities are allocated the appropriate amount of time.

Effective time management guarantees essential personal time and assists you in properly fulfilling your responsibilities. It allows you to set boundaries, prioritise work, and stop putting things off, resulting in more fulfilment and balance. It holds the secret to achieving a genuine work-life balance.

In terms of business, working nonstop without breaks could result in "tunnel vision." Successful entrepreneurs are those who are able to take breaks or outsource less important, smaller jobs to take a step back, see the wider picture, and come back with fresh ideas. It's not just about personal well-being; it is also about making sure the company is innovative and doesn't become stagnant.

Planning, organising, controlling, and making decisions are all crucial components of time management; these activities are also necessary to launch and run a successful business. The goal of time management is to arrange your administrative and business resources so that they maximise their potential and minimise the costs associated with their allocation while producing more output with the same amount of resources.

Time management is essential in daily life to maintain business, planning, task division, and prioritisation. It helps us understand that time is a gift from Allah Almighty, and we must make the most of it. We can accomplish this by using technology and planning how to carry out our responsibilities. The two primary concepts of Islamic teachings are life organisation and planning, and the most crucial and paramount of all is faith in Allah Almighty.

In today's fast-paced society, work and life responsibilities can easily become overwhelming. Many of us struggle to strike a balance between our personal and professional lives, frequently believing that there are not enough hours in the day to get everything done. This is where time management comes in – the art of planning and organising your time to maximise your available hours and accomplish your goals.

Let us delve into the value of time management for achieving a work-life balance and strategies for how you can improve it.

- Prioritise the items on your list by listing them in order of importance. List the highest priorities first, then proceed to the lower ones as time permits.

- Make an effort to create ambitious but attainable goals and divide them into smaller, more doable activities.

- Establish a schedule and take proactive steps to carve out dedicated time for work and personal life.

- Take advantage of the wide range of available time management tools and apps. Utilise calendar software to plan your time, a task management program to monitor your to-do list, and a time monitoring tool to determine how much time you spend on each job. Automation solutions can also help you cut down on the time you invest in administrative tasks by streamlining repeated processes.

Learning the Islamic beauty of professionalism and balance begins with mastering the art of time management. In conclusion, good time management is not just a practical skill but a fundamental component of Islam, as found in the teachings from the Quran and Hadith.

The opening line of Surah Al Asr stresses the significance of time. Through His messenger, Allah (SWT) conveys the message that having enough time is essential to completing your tasks and obligations. And once it is gone, there's no turning back and only regret ahead.

The exemplary life of the Prophet Muhammad (PBUH) serves as a beacon for guidance for humanity. His character, organisation skills, honesty, reliability, and truthfulness are admirable qualities. By embodying these virtues and never engaging in negative discourse, the Prophet demonstrated the value of time.

> *Allah says: "And [they are] those who, when they spend, do so not excessively or sparingly but are ever, between that, [justly] moderate" (Quran 25:67)*

Muslims should rise early in order to enjoy the blessings of Allah and live a prosperous life, as the Prophet Muhammad (SAW) advised:

> *"O Allah, Bless my ummah in the early hours of the morning"* (Ibn Majah)

This hadith makes it abundantly evident that Muslims should prepare for their days early in the morning and get to work. Waking up early for the Fajar prayer is generally a sign from Allah (Almighty), and those who do so may receive benefits from the Almighty. An individual who rises early in the morning has ample time to finish his most critical tasks, which should be completed first.

Integrating spiritual practices (such as *Salah*) into daily routines for productivity

In Islamic entrepreneurship, spiritualities such as Salah are fundamental in improving productivity and providing meaning and relaxation in their careers. "Salah," the Arabic word for daily prayer, denotes an act of adoration unique to Islam in its structure and content. The English term *prayer* conveys a generic feeling of pleading or invocation, while Salah is an act of submission to the Almighty, the creator Allah, and is reflected in a precise and clearly defined physical act that reflects the spirit.

> *According to the Qur'an, "Salah is an obligation on the believers to be observed at its appointed time" (Qur'an 4:103)*

This command requires all individuals who have reached puberty to perform five daily prayers. Additionally, voluntary prayers beyond these obligatory ones are highly encouraged, serving as a recommended practice for seeking divine assistance during times of need.

Beyond what has been mentioned, more prayers are strongly advised as a way to ask God for assistance when things are tough. By performing *salah* several times a day, entrepreneurs develop discipline and harmony, which facilitates productivity and positive thinking for the rest of the day.

> *"And those who strive for us - We will surely guide them to our ways. And indeed, Allah is with the doers of good."*
> (Quran, 29:69)

Including *salah* interruptions within the workweek gives entrepreneurs the time to reflect and recharge while reconnecting with their faith. Short breaks for prayer allow the heads of start-ups to refresh themselves, both physically and mentally, reduce stress, and focus on the work.

Furthermore, *salah* also teaches the need to pray to Allah and seek His help in every task, thus making the mundane aspects of work sacred. The significance of time management and productivity in Islamic entrepreneurship cannot be overemphasised, as productivity entails using time effectively and in harmony with spiritual guidelines.

Chapter Six

Financial Management and Risk-Taking

The principles of Islamic finance for entrepreneurial activities are closer to the principles of ethical behaviour, risk-sharing, and social justice. Let us look at an introduction to Shariah-compliant funding sources and investment techniques for those who are engaged in entrepreneurship and advice on ethical and responsible management of business finances.

Unfavourable outcomes are a necessary component of business operations. Activities that involve the future as it moves through several levels inherently entail uncertainty. Risk is defined as the presence of uncertainty regarding future events.

Conversely, "khatar" and "mukhatarah" were employed by Muslim jurists to refer to business risk. Mukhatarah is defined as the "possibility of unexpected outcomes." When referring to gharar, both khatar and mukhatarah are interchangeable. Muslim business owners must understand how Shariah views various risks and how to manage them to uphold the law's goals.

Risk management is the process of identifying, evaluating, and ranking hazards. It is a planned, cost-effective use of resources to reduce, track, and manage the likelihood and/or consequences of unfavourable occurrences or to optimise the opportunity's realisation.

Risk management aims to ensure that uncertainty does not interfere with the business's aims. Islam's approach to risk management is based on the Quran and Sunnah.

Islamic Finance Principles for Entrepreneurial Ventures

A form of financing known as Islamic finance is subject to Sharia (Islamic Law). The idea can also be used to discuss investments that comply with Sharia law. The primary distinction between conventional and Islamic banking lies in that some techniques and ideas utilised in the former are categorically forbidden by Sharia law. Sharia law is closely adhered to by Islamic finance. The foundation of modern Islamic banking is a set of rules that are not always against the law in the nations where Islamic financial institutions operate:

- In Islam, certain acts are forbidden, such as making and selling alcohol or meat. These activities are prohibited or deemed haram. It is, therefore, prohibited to invest in such enterprises.

- Islam views interest-bearing loans as exploitative practices that benefit the lender at the borrower's expense. Interest is considered usury (riba) under Sharia law and is strictly forbidden.

- Islamic finance regulations forbid participating in transactions with great risk or ambiguity. The legitimacy of uncertainty or risk in investments is gauged by the term "gharar." Contracts for derivatives and short sales are examples of harar, which are prohibited in Islamic finance.

- Sharia forbids *maisir*, or speculation and gambling, in all its forms. Islamic financial institutions, therefore, cannot be parties to agreements in which the ownership of the products is contingent upon an unclear future event.

The call for a reasonable and equitable system that is sustainable and socially conscious is growing, as is awareness of Islamic banking and finance.

> *"There will come a time when one will have no concern about how one gains one's money, whether legally or illegally," prophesied the Prophet (Bukhari)*

Thus, adhering to Islamic principles, individuals seek to distance themselves from the disregard of ethical concerns. This necessitates a return to the foundational principles guiding Islamic teachings.

Islamic banking, in its essence, promotes entrepreneurship and commerce while forbidding interest in all commercial transactions, citing the Quranic passage.

> *"Allah has permitted trade and has forbidden riba (interest)" (Qur'an 2:275)*

Overview of Sharia-compliant financing options and investment strategies

Islamic commercial financing serves the needs of individuals who want to run their businesses according to the Sharia laws. Mudarabah, a profit-sharing venture in which one party contributes funds (Rab al-Mal) and the other contributes efforts and management (Mudarib), is one of the most utilised forms of Sharia-compliant financing.

Another type of Shariah-compliant financing is Musharakah, in which both parties contribute to the financing, assets, and liabilities, and profit and losses are shared based on the agreed-upon ratios. Musharakah serves to distribute risks and encourages active participation from both the entrepreneur and the investor.

Apart from equity-based financing, there are other Islamic debt securities, such as Sukuk, an Islamic bond formed under Sharia law. Sukuks are Islamic bonds used to finance tangible assets, and the Sukuk holders have rights in those assets and an income proportional to their performance.

Managing business finances ethically and responsibly

Ethical and responsible management of business finances is necessary for Islamic entrepreneurship, which adheres to Sharia laws. Entrepreneurs must be honest, ethical, and socially responsible with their finances.

The other significant concept of Islamic finance is the prohibition of riba, commonly known as interest-based transactions, which are prohibited by Islamic law. Business owners can look for other legal means of financing prohibited in Sharia but can otherwise be used to finance business development, such as Murabaha or Ijara.

Finally, Muslim entrepreneurs should be fiscally cautious when engaging in their activities and steer clear of undue risk-taking. Implementing measures to reduce risks, manage cash flow, and secure future profits is essential for suitable business growth. This requires adopting appropriate financial management practices and exercising financial responsibility at all times.

Balancing Risk and Reward in Islamic Entrepreneurship

Unfavourable outcomes are inevitable aspects of business operations. Any activities that involve forecasting future events inherently involve uncertainty at various levels. Risk, by definition, arises from this uncertainty regarding future events. In business, risk stems from the unpredictability that comes with a company's or an individual's line of work. This unpredictability can manifest in factors such as fluctuating input costs or future sales, all of which impact the product market.

Financial risk is the uncertainty brought on by potential losses in the financial markets due to changes in financial variables, such as interest rates, stock prices, commodity prices, and currency rates. Every business organisation that operates in an ever-changing atmosphere must have an active risk mitigation plan to safeguard itself against unforeseen outcomes.

Effective risk management is the management's primary duty and should be integrated into the corporate governance framework as a whole. The components of an efficient risk management system include risk identification, measurement, monitoring, and limitation. In turn, these processes rely on suitable auditing and control protocols. We will talk about risk management briefly in the following section.

Evaluating business risks through the lens of Islamic principles

In Islam, risk management is acceptable. The management method must align with Shariah principles as it entails safeguarding individuals and their belongings against potential loss. It views hifz al-mal, or the protection of wealth, as a value that is highly valued in Islam.

Risk is acceptable from an Islamic standpoint, unlike gharar, which is forbidden. According to one of the hadiths of the Prophet Muhammad (PBUH), it is impossible to dispute another person's safety or property, and any infringement on another person's rights is considered a property crime. The Prophet (PBUH) also advocated for sharing economic risks to split gains and losses and fostering cooperation and mutual support.

For example, the musharakah product is founded on a joint venture and capital cooperation. Every employee in the company contributes to the capital and shares in the company's gains and losses. The entrepreneurs (mudharib) and investors (rabbul mal) split the profit and loss on mudharabah products. Even when investors only contribute capital and entrust the company's management to its operators, they are not entitled to compensate in the case of a risk or business failure brought on by an operator's unintentional negligence.

Risk analysis for Islamic entrepreneurship focuses on evaluating the strengths, weaknesses, opportunities, and threats of managing business activities conforming to the Islamic Shariah, which addresses equity and ethical behaviour. Risk assessment is conducted with reverence and humility, bearing in mind that the success of the venture depends on Allah.

Chapter Seven

Social Impact and Community Engagement

Islamic entrepreneurship entails social responsibility, which emphasises entrepreneurs' moral duties toward the betterment of the community. This section examines how Islamic entrepreneurship is centred on community development, supply chain integrity, and sustainability.

Social Responsibility in Islamic Entrepreneurship

The core tenet of corporate social responsibility (CSR) is that businesses are responsible for promoting societal progress. It is said that the corporate organisation only survives because it provides for important societal demands.

In Islam, conducting business is regarded as a religious duty. The term "social responsibility" describes an organisation's duties to uphold and improve the society in which it operates. By sharing affluence for the advancement of society, the ideas of social justice and brotherhood give rise to civic duty. As a result, CSR is seen as essential to consider for Islamic commercial enterprises.

Innovating for Community Development and Societal Well-Being in Business

Islamic entrepreneurship focuses on the role played by businesses in promoting the welfare of societies and communities. As stated, start-up initiatives should pinpoint social issues and create products and services to tackle them, including poverty, illiteracy, diseases, and pollution.

An example of ways that entrepreneurs can support the development of communities is through performing the act of Zakat, which is known as the form of compulsory charity in Islam. Entrepreneurs can contribute their profits to Zakat-eligible causes to help those in need, provide basic needs to underserved populations, and foster the spirit of economic enfranchisement.

In addition, they can continue to generate employment, foster skills acquisition, and enhance people's capacities through training and development. If organisations focus on hiring human resources and developing business enterprises within the societies, they will contribute positively to the economy's growth, unemployment, and poverty.

Ethical Supply Chains and Sustainable Actions

Ethical supply chain management and sustainability are important to Islamic entrepreneurs, who suggest justice, fairness, and stewardship as key values to be upheld when conducting business. The guidelines also encourage ethical sourcing and treatment of workers and call on entrepreneurs to reduce the negative impact on the environment at different stages of the supply chain.

One way of encouraging an ethical supply chain is through halal certifications, which certify that food products adhere to Islamic dietary laws and standards. Working with halal-certified suppliers and producers enables business owners to uphold trust and act responsibly, meeting the expectations of both consumers and fellow businesses when selecting products.

In addition, entrepreneurs are encouraged to use practices that do not harm the environment, consume fewer resources, and produce less waste. This way, through the adoption of green energy, emissions cuts, and environmentally friendly measures, corporate entities can be part of the solution to environmental degradation while improving efficiency, sustainability, and operating profits in the long run.

CSR is one of the crucial components that should facilitate the development of societies and communities in the framework of Islamic entrepreneurship. The potential for value creation can be achieved by focusing on ethical supply chains, sustainable business models, and what positive impacts might be delivered to the communities that the businesses serve or disrupt. Therefore, in their businesses, young entrepreneurs may find Islamic law useful when handling corporate social responsibility programs and forming ethical and responsible business cultures.

Building Stronger Communities Through Entrepreneurship

In this respect, they have the economic opportunity to revolutionise society, protect the endangered parties of the population, and provide for the general welfare. Let us identify how entrepreneurship contributes to social development mainly through buying local products, engaging the disadvantaged in society and partnering with other members of the society for better lives.

Discovering a community of support can mean the difference between quitting after the first setback and creating the next game-changer. Furthermore, community is crucial on all fronts, within a team or throughout a whole region. Creating a prosperous entrepreneurial community is not easy, but once established, things can move quite swiftly in that direction.

A community's odds of success for new businesses increase when it fosters a thriving ecosystem of successful businesses. This not only attracts more talent and investment but also inspires the upcoming generation of business owners to locate their startup companies there.

Establishing economies of scale for common needs results in financial benefits when the concentration of startups in a given location increases. Finally, as the number of profitable companies rises regularly, seasoned business owners start to give back to the community by supplying invaluable information and expertise, repurposed funds, and mentorship opportunities. A crucial element of becoming an entrepreneur is acknowledging and even celebrating failure. Very few business owners are successful with their first venture or concept.

And many people who possess all the necessary qualities to succeed as high-achieving business owners encounter their first setback before giving up. It is a terrible pity, and once more, surrounding yourself with the right people can make all the difference.

Here's where the community comes into play. As individuals, we are susceptible to internal recriminations and self-doubt when things do not work out. But if we have the correct support system and community behind us, we may start to view failure as a necessary step on the path to achievement rather than as the destination in and of itself.

Sustaining Local Economy and Enhancing the Status of Minorities through Business Ventures

The concept of entrepreneurship plays a crucial role in economic growth and the advancement of local communities. Entrepreneurs create new employment opportunities which boost economic development and revenue circulation in specific regions of the economy.

Also, entrepreneurship can positively impact society by providing opportunities to otherwise excluded individuals such as females, youths, minorities, and refugees. These groups can only regain their economic narratives by participating in entrepreneurship training, mentorship, and funding from the communities.

Self-generated entrepreneurs also help solve specific communities' issues and meet the needs of vulnerable people. These innovative businesspeople devise out-of-the-box strategies that seek to solve social problems and enhance the quality of life and social integration in society from their cultural and local vantage points.

Working with the community members for the common good

Entrepreneurship is one of the most powerful tools for building stronger communities. To achieve this goal, various stakeholders, including state and non-governmental organisations, educational institutions, and companies, have to work in partnership. Together, these stakeholders can harness their capital, knowledge, and contacts to foster an environment conducive to entrepreneurship and economic growth.

Community members can encourage the growth of entrepreneurship by offering programs that offer support structures and funding to entrepreneurs, including incubators, accelerators, and business development organisations. Also, through relationships with local governments, one can encourage legislation changes and the provision of infrastructures and public services that may help foster business engagements.

In addition, working with academic institutions can help spread entrepreneurship knowledge, skills, and research that fosters a culture of innovation and entrepreneurship within communities. Stakeholders must promote innovation, experience, competition, and risk-taking to generate chances for mutual benefit and long-term success.

Despite this, the prospects for entrepreneurship that may positively affect the development of communities and economies and give a chance to socially excluded populations are promising. Thus, communities can promote meaningful programs and structures through which members can pursue economic improvement, mobility, and sustainable growth. This can only mean that as people come together and help nurture the environment for business, they can achieve the best for the people and help improve society for the better.

Chapter Eight

Networking and Collaborative Partnerships

Bridges formation is critical to Islamic entrepreneurship, emphasising trustful, genuine, and reciprocal partnerships. Establishing a solid network is essential to your business's success as a Muslim entrepreneur. Maintaining your religious and cultural beliefs while securing new economic chances and expanding your knowledge are all made possible through networking. Networking is more crucial than ever in today's fast-paced business world, and those who ignore it risk missing out on significant chances to expand their companies.

Importance of Relationship Building in Islamic Entrepreneurship

Connecting with other Muslim professionals and business owners is one of the main advantages of business networking for Muslim entrepreneurs. These connections can be a great source of inspiration, fresh ideas, and views as you develop your company.

As a Muslim entrepreneur, you can share expertise, cooperate on initiatives, and work towards common objectives. By tapping into these networks, you gain access to priceless resources like capital, coaching, and guidance from seasoned industry professionals. These tools can assist you in overcoming obstacles, expanding your company, and accomplishing your objectives.

Attending social gatherings and connecting with other professionals and entrepreneurs who identify as Muslim will open doors to new possibilities for business that you might not have otherwise known about. You will be able to keep ahead of your rivals and make smarter judgments by learning about the most recent trends and advancements in your business.

Business networking involves giving back to society as well as gaining advantages. By imparting your knowledge and skills, you strengthen bonds with people and contribute to their success. This reciprocal exchange fosters inspiration and motivation, keeping you focused on your objectives.

One of the most important factors in Muslim entrepreneurs' success is business networking. It offers connections with other Muslim professionals and entrepreneurs, access to vital resources, a chance to give back to the community, and enhanced visibility and reputation.

To fully capitalise on these opportunities, as an entrepreneur, you should be sincere, join online forums, attend networking events, and maintain focus on your goals. By leveraging the benefits of business networking, you can grow your company and positively impact your community.

Networking with integrity and sincerity to create meaningful connections

If you are an entrepreneur or want to launch your own company, networking is essential to the success of your enterprise. Here are some ways that networking might help you in your entrepreneurial path:

Integrity is one of the most crucial components of a successful networking strategy. Honest and forthright people tend to attract others. Being sincere and taking an authentic approach to conversations are crucial when networking. Share your experiences, passions, and interests in a way that authentically represents you. Openness creates the foundation for meaningful interactions by fostering trust. Remember that "people connect with people" extends beyond job designations and achievements.

Assisting one another is the essence of networking. That is the skill of figuring out how to give back. Seek opportunities to help others, impart your skills, or establish connections with individuals in your network. Being willing to lend a hand to others fosters a good atmosphere that strengthens bonds. Additionally, you demonstrate that you care about the success of those around you and your competence in what you do when you assist others in succeeding.

In summary, the key to successful networking is sincerity and honesty. It is more important to have a network of people who genuinely support and encourage one another than it is to have a large number of connections. Gaining proficiency in networking will enable you to collaborate with others, create new opportunities, and succeed in both your personal and professional life.

Fostering collaborative partnerships for business growth and impact

In the contemporary business world, collaborative partnerships are crucial for a number of strong reasons. In today's dynamic and ever-evolving corporate environment, cooperative alliances have become essential to success. When executed correctly, collaboration offers a number of benefits and can significantly increase employee engagement, productivity, and well-being. The three key components of a successful collaborative organisation are clear goals, appropriate technologies, and a collaborative company culture.

In your business environment, collaboration refers to you or your team working towards a shared goal or purpose. You and your team can collaborate to achieve a short-term goal. However, when collaboration becomes ingrained in your entire company, long-term partnerships become imperative. To cultivate a collaborative work environment, you must facilitate the sustained exchange of diverse ideas and skill sets.

The Advantages of Teamwork

Enhanced invention: Collaboration creates an atmosphere favourable to invention by bringing together a variety of viewpoints, abilities, and resources. Companies might obtain novel technology, concepts, and methods through collaborations that might not be accessible within their own company.

Market Expansion: Through partnerships, businesses can reach a wider range of customers and penetrate new markets. Businesses can explore unexplored areas by utilising each other's networks, distribution routes, and skills through strategic alliances.

Risk Mitigation: Through strategic alliances, businesses can pool resources and share risks, which can be especially helpful in industries that are unstable or very competitive. Companies that work together with similar organisation s can overcome obstacles and adjust to changes in their business environment.

Cost Efficiency: Cooperative activities frequently result in cost savings by pooling resources, taking advantage of economies of scale, and making joint investments. This can be particularly helpful for tiny businesses trying to compete with bigger ones.

Partnerships are very important in Islamic entrepreneurship as they help expand businesses and provide services to society. The history of entrepreneurship also underlines the importance of identifying and engaging potential partners with similar visions and objectives.

Strategic partnerships can be of different types, such as strategic partnerships, joint ventures, and co-creation ventures. The parties must utilise collective resources, specialised knowledge, and connections to counter emerging obstacles, capture opportunities, and pursue common goals.

Entrepreneurs can also increase their initiative reach and effectiveness in the community through partnerships. These organisations, charities, and influential members of society can help entrepreneurs implement their ideas, solve social problems, spur economic growth, and improve society's well-being.

Muslim entrepreneurs and organisations' cooperation is vital in spearheading change and advancements within the Muslim and overall society. This section provides examples of successful collaborations involving the joint use of resources described below.

Analysis of Effective Muslim Businesspeople Collaborations

Finance availability is also limited in many Muslim-majority countries, especially for young, budding entrepreneurs from marginalised backgrounds. The Microfinance and Entrepreneurship Development Program (MEDP) is a project involving the Islamic banking industry and non-governmental and governmental organisations. Its aim is to offer micro-financing and entrepreneurship education for those in need.

MEDP provides microloans and business training together with mentorship to startups or emerging entrepreneurs. Specifically, MEDP has incorporated both Mudarabah and Musharakah to help entrepreneurs obtain capital through Islamic finance solutions to foster economic development and fight poverty.

Halal Food Distribution Network

Halal food supply chains involve the producers, distributors, sellers, and buyers of halal foods, making halal products available in the local and global markets. These networks comprise collaboration between halal certification organisations, food manufacturers, transporters, and sellers to enhance the food chains and satisfy the increasing consumer demand for halal food.

It will also show how supply chain relationships impact market coverage, product quality conventions and halal compliance. These partnerships help expand the halal industry, generate employment and increase consumer confidence and trust in certified halal products.

Engaging Collective Capital and Talent for Social and Economic Advancement

Islamic Social Finance Initiatives

Islamic social finance instruments, including Waqf (endowment), Zakat (compulsory charity) and Sadaqah (voluntary charity), mobilise donor/charitable individuals and institutions, philanthropic organisations and communities for social and economic needs. These initiatives combine funds to support causes such as education, health, poverty eradication, and other charitable causes. In this sense, Islamic social finance can transform, socially empower the deprived, support developmental projects, and enhance social solidarity within communities.

Technology Incubators and Accelerators

Technology incubators and accelerators offer resources, guidance, and capital to technology startups and early-stage companies. These initiatives entail collaborations between universities, the government, venture capitalists, and industry professionals to support innovation and start-ups.

Through pooling resources and talent, technology incubation/acceleration ecosystems provide a conducive environment for entrepreneurial businesses, the growth and development of disruptive technologies, and economic growth and employment.

Muslims collectively need to support each other to contribute towards positive change and social and economic transformation. Muslim entrepreneurs can solve multi-faceted problems, create additional value, and positively change the world through such practical examples of successful collaborations and the effective utilisation of resources and knowledge. More businesspeople form partnerships for better results; let them be inspired by various successful partnership and cooperation examples for the greater good of society and a better economy.

Chapter Nine

Future Trends in Islamic Entrepreneurship

The global halal economy offers significant business opportunities for Islamic entrepreneurs due to changes in consumer behaviour, new technology, and variations in the market structure. Now, it is time to examine recent trends and opportunities that define the direction of the development of Islamic entrepreneurship in building the prospects for innovative technological solutions for sustainable business development in the context of the halal economy.

Current Trends and Markets Influencing Islamic Entrepreneurial Development

Rise of Muslim Consumerism: As the number of Muslims increases, their purchasing power and knowledge regarding halal options have also increased, prompting the growth in various halal markets such as food, finance, tourism, clothing, and even cosmetics. Entrepreneurs have an opportunity to capitalise on this trend by introducing new products and services that cater to the needs and expectations of Muslims in different countries.

Halal Tourism and Hospitality: Halal tourism is gradually becoming popular as more travellers seek destinations that accommodate their Islamic beliefs. To capitalise on this, the hospitality industry should target this market by providing Islamic-friendly hotels and resorts and travel agencies that cater to the needs of Muslim tourists.

Halal Finance and Fintech: Islamic finance and fintech are on the rise and have opportunities for further expansion as more individuals and organisations seek out Islamic financial services. Entrepreneurs may find various areas of interest within this sector, including halal banking, Islamic investment funds, peer-to-peer lending markets, and halal digital payment systems oriented towards the needs of the Muslim population and businesses.

Ethical and Sustainable Consumption: Muslim consumers have increasingly become conscious of their purchase decisions and their impact on society and the world through ethical and sustainable consumption. Marketing strategies could be used to tackle these issues, as consumers are placing more importance on brand attributes such as transparency in the supply chain, environmentally friendly products and socially responsible businesses.

Harnessing Innovation and Technology for Sustainable Business Growth

By utilising digital technologies' potential, businesses can create strong and resilient approaches that help them prosper in the face of rapid cultural change and global uncertainty. As the world changes, entrepreneurs must adapt to these principles to stay competitive, foster innovation, and guarantee long-term success.

With sustainability emerging as a key component of business strategy, the technology developments mentioned below are essential to implementing sustainable practices.

E-commerce and Digital Platforms: Technological advancement, specifically in the area of e-commerce and online platforms, has significantly transformed the process of marketing and selling halal products and services. Internet channels consist of online markets, mobile applications, and social media networks to market to consumers and enable effective buying processes in the contemporary world.

Blockchain and Traceability: By adopting blockchain technology, the halal supply chain benefits from increased transparency and traceability, allowing consumers to confirm the genuineness and purity of halal goods. This technology records the journey of halal products, from production to consumption, ensuring compliance with halal standards as well as increasing consumer confidence.

Agri-tech and Food Innovation: Innovative agricultural technologies, including vertical farming, precision agriculture, and sustainable food production methods, are expected to impact the halal food sector. In halal food production, these technologies can be employed to improve food security, enhance nutritional value and reduce environmental impact in response to the increasing global demand for healthy and sustainable foods.

Smart Cities and Halal Infrastructure: As urban areas evolve into smart cities, there is an increasing need to address the diverse needs of Muslim urban residents. This creates unlimited opportunities for Muslim entrepreneurs to engage in smart city projects through the infusion of halal facilities, services, and amenities. By doing so, they can make smart city projects more inclusive and accommodating to Muslims.

In light of new trends, technology, and consumer preferences, the global halal economy offers business opportunities for Islamic entrepreneurship. By exploring market trends and adapting to innovation and technology for business sustainability, entrepreneurs can take advantage of more of these opportunities and assist in developing a competitive global halal economy. When charting the course of their businesses in the future as Islamic businessmen and women, they should consider embracing innovation, flexibility, and positive thinking to realise the potential of the new dispensation.

Sustaining the Islamic Entrepreneurship Mindset for Long-Term Success

Once the Islamic entrepreneurship mindset is cultivated, it needs to be sustained to improve business conditions, enhance knowledge, and ensure the succession of future generations. This section will discuss the measures that should be taken and the strategies that should be implemented to ensure the future sustainability of the Islamic entrepreneurship mindset.

Strategies for Lifelong Learning, Change, and Development in Businesses

In these highly disruptive times, entrepreneurs need to continue learning new skills to increase their knowledge, skills, and competencies. The urgency of work often trumps the luxury of learning. Learning should fit within the flow of daily work life so that learning can occur within busy schedules. Finding opportunities to learn "on the job" and "in the job" is a practical way to accelerate lifelong learning in organisations.

Ultimately, it is up to the entrepreneurs to cultivate the right mindset; a "growth mindset" is a good place to start, especially in an environment where learning never ends. Businesses with a growth mentality reward learning from mistakes and promote taking reasonable risks. They facilitate cross-organisational collaboration and increase accessibility and availability of learning. Prosperous businesses discover methods to integrate education into the routine of their employees' workdays.

Entrepreneurs with a growth mentality think that hard work, sound tactics, and advice from others may help them develop their talents. To become lifelong learners, entrepreneurs must first think they have the opportunity and limitless potential to learn and develop.

The significance of lifelong learning must be considered in today's fast-paced, highly digital business environment. Talent professionals and leaders are acutely aware that the knowledge and skills of today may not meet the needs of tomorrow.

To be flexible and agile, one must repeatedly learn, reconsider, and relearn. This is the essence of lifelong learning. It is a persistent challenge that compels the re-evaluation of established learning paradigms and the cultivation of a culture of constant learning and adaptability within organisations.

Nowadays, routine activities are increasingly automated, creating a growing demand for individuals with stronger cognitive, artistic, and interpersonal abilities. The nature of labour has altered significantly as a result of the digital revolution's capabilities in automation, machine learning, and artificial intelligence.

Effective tactics for promoting lifelong learning include microlearning, learning sprints, instant learning materials, and mentoring. Furthermore, machine learning and artificial intelligence technology can create flexible learning environments that can be tailored to each student's needs and learning style.

It's common for businesses to mistakenly view lifelong learning solely as a tool for professional growth. However, it's crucial to keep in mind that continuous education also involves personal growth, encouraging inquisitiveness, introspection, and resilience. This strategy cultivates an adaptable mindset, which is necessary in today's turbulent workplace.

Nowadays, businesses enhance learning outcomes by allowing their staff members the freedom to choose materials that best suit their interests, learning preferences, and professional objectives. This approach makes employees feel more engaged in their education, which promotes better knowledge retention and application.

Leaders need to set an example by embracing lifelong learning and being advocates for it. They ought to emphasise the value of education and demonstrate how it directly affects performance as a whole. They create an atmosphere that is conducive to lifelong learning by encouraging a growth mentality. This effort gains credibility and influence among staff members when they witness leaders actively engaging in and promoting learning.

The encouragement of information exchange within the company is another important component that prompts lifelong learning. Creating channels for staff members to exchange ideas and pick up tips from one another can greatly increase the organisation's collective knowledge base.

This can be facilitated through social learning platforms, online discussion boards, or mentoring programs, among other things. These initiatives streamline knowledge sharing and foster a sense of connectivity and collaboration among employees.

The next stage involves incorporating learning into regular work tasks. This can be achieved by developing educational opportunities that are closely related to the work in question, like project-based learning, job rotation, and on-the-job training.

By incorporating learning into their regular work activities, employees can immediately apply and strengthen the understanding they have received. This "learn while you work" approach closes the knowledge gap between acquisition and application by making learning more approachable and immediately useful.

The last step is to use technological resources and platforms to provide readily available, personalised, and adaptive learning. With the help of AI and data analytics, organisations can measure progress, give timely feedback, and obtain greater insight into learning behaviours.

These technological interventions improve the effectiveness, interactivity, and engagement of learning. Additionally, they enable organisations to customise instruction to meet the needs of each student, optimising learning results and improving the quality of the educational process as a whole.

Embracing lifelong learning is crucial for the nurturing and sustenance of the Islamic entrepreneurship mindset. Self-employed individuals should continuously seek to enhance their skills in relation to the changing techniques, products and market conditions. This can be done by attending workshops, conferences, online classes or seeking consultation from other professionals in the given field to expand knowledge and ideas.

The journey to sustain the Islamic entrepreneurship mindset is not an easy one, as there are bound to be challenges and failures. However, adopting a mindset that recognises challenges as opportunities for growth is essential. By embracing optimism, a positive time perspective, and drawing on faith and spirituality, it is possible to overcome failure and persevere as an entrepreneur.

Encouraging lifelong learning makes personnel flexible, agile, and prepared to step into the next organisational void. Lifelong learning creates the foundation for success in the workplace today, both now and in the future.

Advancing the Legacy of Islamic Entrepreneurship for Future Generations

In the past, Muslims leveraged scientific and technological advancement to construct a greater civilisation and attain sufficient welfare to achieve high standards of living. Today, Muslims find themselves in a variety of economic circumstances based on where they reside.

One of the primary drivers of growth that would allow Muslim communities to meet their demands for a greater standard of living is entrepreneurship. Since Islam greatly emphasises it, it has also been included in Islamic religious instruction. Muslims have practised entrepreneurship from the time of the Holy Prophet Muhammad (PBUH). The young Prophet's early entrepreneurial endeavours gave him many of his management and leadership abilities as an orphan.

> *Allah says: And when the Prayer is finished, then may disperse through the land, and seek of the Bounty of Allah: and celebrate the Praises of Allah often (and without stint): that ye may prosper (Quran 62:10)*

After prayer, there is a reference to seeking Allah's bounty, suggesting that working is necessary and accepted as a component of Muslim life in addition to worship.

Encouraging Muslim leaders to prioritise the development of future Muslim generations with a strong entrepreneurial spirit is vital. This can be achieved through launching tailored training and mentorship initiatives for young people focused on core entrepreneurial principles.

These initiatives can be competitive-based, where young students can launch enterprises based on their ideas at the next level with financial assistance from the public and private sectors. The primary goal of these initiatives should be to instill an entrepreneurial culture in the university environment so that staff members, instructors, and students can voluntarily profit from entrepreneurship in many aspects of their daily lives. Moreover, measures should be taken to advance the legacy of Islamic entrepreneurship for future generations.

Lead by Example: Islamic entrepreneurs can continue the tradition of Islamic entrepreneurship through this role-modelling behaviour and by practising integrity, ethics, and other socially responsible behaviours in their businesses. By showing this positive correlation between Islamic values and business success, these role models encourage future generations to follow the Islamic entrepreneurship disposition and incorporate these values in their ventures.

Mentorship and Knowledge Sharing: Training upcoming business individuals and providing knowledge and experiences are among the most effective means to help build on the legacy of Islamic entrepreneurship. Mentorship is another way entrepreneurs can contribute to the development of young professionals, students, and other aspiring entrepreneurs by offering advice and encouragement. In the same respect, entrepreneurs can further support knowledge-sharing through workshops, seminars, or educational activities to pass on important information and lessons to Islamic business aspirants.

Support Entrepreneurial Ecosystems: Promoting and developing an entrepreneurial ecosystem is crucial to achieving a suitable environment for Islamic entrepreneurship. Industry associations, incubators, accelerators, and government agencies are some of the key stakeholders that can be joined to champion policies and programs that support entrepreneurship, innovation, and economic growth.

For Islamic entrepreneurship to be sustained in the long run, the principles must continue to be learnt and implemented throughout the generations to ensure that the great legacy of Islamic entrepreneurship is kept alive.

Therefore, by promoting lifelong learning, innovation, and resilience, as well as by setting an example, providing guidance, and fostering support structures for budding entrepreneurs, the tenets of Islamic entrepreneurship can endure and prosper for centuries to come. May the spirit of innovation and hard work among entrepreneurs never wane as they run their businesses, embracing the tenets of Islamic Shariah as beacons and shining examples for the younger generation to emulate!

Chapter Ten

Final Thoughts

As we conclude our exploration of Muslimpreneur mindset, we are reminded that success isn't about happiness, money, or power; success is making a difference in the world. Over the course of this process, we have explored the Islamic model of entrepreneurship and outlined a philosophy that posits loyalty, empathy, and corporate responsibility as core factors to business success.

As we have seen, becoming an entrepreneur is a difficult, thrilling, and frequently unpredictable path. To develop something fresh and valuable, one needs vision, guts, and perseverance. As an entrepreneur, you may encounter additional moral conundrums while trying to strike a balance between Islamic principles and material success. So far, our focus has been on how to apply Islamic concepts to business endeavours, cultivating a mindset that fosters success through vision and religion without sacrificing integrity, morals, or convictions.

The world of entrepreneurship is full of obstacles and hard times. Upholding and putting into practice the fundamental Islamic ideals and values is crucial, as is maintaining a positive outlook and resilient mindset in the face of the demands of both personal and professional achievement. As a successful entrepreneur, you are expected to conduct yourself with the utmost ethics in all that you do. This entails carrying out all of your actions with integrity, equity, respect, and compassion. Your moral values should never be compromised for the sake of your achievement.

It is your duty as an entrepreneur to uphold the highest moral standards as you pursue your goals. Make an effort to improve the world via your endeavours and keep your morals and beliefs at the centre of your business decisions. To sum up, balancing material goals with spiritual fulfilment is necessary to integrate Islamic teachings with business. It entails conducting business to benefit people, add value, and improve society.

From the linkage between faith and entrepreneurship to visionary leadership rooted in divine guidance, this book has presented several Islamic principles relevant to today's multifaceted and highly competitive business environment. From the examples of people's experiences, inspire and learn how faith can help overcome and shift towards a successful life.

We have highlighted the rationale for ethical behaviour at the workplace, noting that integrity, reliability, and objectivity are not mere virtues to aspire to but are vital prerequisites for any organisation's success and the well-being of society. This has shown how the Islamic values of entrepreneurship can create economically and socially viable businesses that positively impact society.

In this process, we have highlighted the virtues of stakeholder involvement and coalitions, acknowledging that change is not an individual process but a concerted effort based on the principles of partnership. As entrepreneurs, our platforms afford us the opportunity to scale up and spread positivity by fostering genuine, trust-based business relationships.

Looking ahead, we find endless possibilities for the advancement and diversification of the halal economy worldwide. By embracing the principles of Islamic entrepreneurship and maintaining the perspective of faith and vision, we can pave the way for a successful future driven by entrepreneurial spirit and the desire to make a positive change.

This is more than a book; it's an appeal, a challenge to open a new chapter in the book of business success. Whether you are an experienced entrepreneur or a startup founder, I urge you to move forward with the knowledge you have gained, guided by the principles of faith, honesty, and mercy as values.

May you succeed in all your endeavours, Allah (swt) willing, and may all your undertakings help make the world better for future generations. I thank you for being part of this process, and I hope your businesses will be a source of inspiration and joy.

Find Out More

Website: www.barakahinbusiness.com

Socials: @barakahinbusiness

If you enjoyed this book, kindly leave a review to help expand our reach so others may benefit also.

www.ingramcontent.com/pod-product-compliance
Lightning Source LLC
Chambersburg PA
CBHW070432010526
44118CB00014B/2017